Ecumenism:

Another Gospel

Lausanne's Road to Rome

ES Williams

Belmont House Publishing

London

Ecumenism: Another Gospel
Lausanne's Road to Rome
is published by Belmont House Publishing

First published   February 2014

ISBN 0 9548493 8 8

Scripture quotations from the New King James Version, unless otherwise indicated. Copyright 1982, Thomas Nelson, Inc. Used by permission.

Published by Belmont House Publishing
36 The Crescent
Belmont
SUTTON
Surrey SM2 6BJ

Website www.belmonthouse.co.uk

A Catalogue record for this book is available from the British Library.

Ecumenism: Another Gospel
Lausanne's Road to Rome

Table of contents:

Preface

The Lausanne Movement, created by two of the most well known Christian leaders of the day, evangelist Billy Graham and theologian John Stott, was ostensibly established to further the cause of world evangelization. In his opening address to Christian leaders gathered together for the first Lausanne Congress (1974), the famous evangelist said it could be the most significant gathering in the history of the Christian Church. He boldly declared that 'evangelism has taken on a new meaning'. And so in the space of ten days church leaders became convinced that the Gospel message of salvation needed to be combined with social and political action. John Stott explained that evangelism and social action are like two blades of a pair of scissors or two wings of a bird.

The first Lausanne Congress was undoubtedly a defining moment in the history of the Church, for evangelism had indeed taken on a new meaning. The Lausanne Covenant, written largely by John Stott, described this new approach, using the term 'evangelization', to emphasise the importance of a Christian commitment to the cause of social justice. Over the years the Lausanne approach to evangelism has exerted a great influence on churches, para-church organisations and missionary organisations worldwide.

Lausanne II in Manila in 1989, strongly influenced by charismatic ideas and styles of worship, produced numerous strategic partnerships that emphasised the need for cooperation with the Church of Rome in ethical issues, social work and political action so long as the biblical Gospel was not compromised.

Lausanne III in Cape Town in 2010 saw the gathering of over four thousand Christian leaders from across the world, with some of the biggest names in evangelicalism, such as Pastor John Piper, Rev Nicky Gumbell and Dr Tim Keller, as keynote speakers. By now the ecumenical agenda of Lausanne was plain for all to see, as the Congress was addressed by the General Secretary of the World Council of Churches. The cry was for unity in love, as doctrinal differences were set to one side.

Ecumenism: Another Gospel is an examination of the Lausanne Movement from its first Congress in 1974 to the Cape Town gathering in 2010. And while it may be difficult for some believers to accept that an organisation established by two of the most influential Christian leaders of our time is promoting a compromised socio-political gospel, I ask readers serious about contending for the faith to carefully and patiently examine the evidence presented in these pages. Bible believing Christians who truly care about the Gospel of Truth will be deeply disturbed, as I was, by the messages and practices that are coming from this Movement.

Over four decades the socio-political agenda of Lausanne has become increasingly overt, as issues such as global warming, world poverty and women's leadership have become centre stage. Even more worrying is the growth in ecumenism, and an acceptance of the ways and thinking of the emerging church. But perhaps that greatest sign that all is not right within Lausanne is its enthusiastic promotion of the orality movement and the so-called 'oral Bible', that down plays the importance of God's written Word.

What is so disturbing about the Lausanne compromise described in these pages is that it is misleading Christians in the developing world, and subverting the message of missionary organisations across the globe.

ES Williams

Sincere thanks to my brothers in Christ, Michael de Semlyen and Graham Parkhouse, who helped improve this manuscript with their wise counsel.

Chapter 1

The Cause of World Evangelization

The Lausanne Committee for World Evangelization, commonly referred to as Lausanne, is an international movement that seeks to energise churches, mission agencies, networks and individuals to respond with vigour and courage to the cause of world evangelization. It is the single largest and most influential institution in evangelical Christianity in the world today—a truly international movement with support from most countries across the globe. For the last four decades, under the Lausanne banner, Christian leaders have participated in regional, national and international consultations, seminars and conferences to develop strategic approaches to evangelise the world.

The third Lausanne Congress in Cape Town in October 2010 was held in collaboration with the World Evangelical Alliance. It brought together around four thousand leaders from 197 countries. According to Douglas Birdsall, Lausanne's Executive Chair, 'These leaders, carefully chosen from thousands of applicants, will represent the demographic, theological and cultural realities of the global Church. Young and old, men and women, mission leaders, pastors and theologians, Kingdom-minded leaders from the worlds of business, government, education, medicine and the media – the Congress is drawing the best minds and most creative and courageous leaders the Church has to offer.'[1] Over six hundred global link sites were connected with the Congress in ninety-one countries, and the internet made it possible for many thousands of people to follow the main sessions of the Congress. In his opening address Douglas Birdsall said, 'This third Lausanne Congress has already been described as the most representative and diverse gathering of Christian leaders in the nearly 2000-year history of the Christian movement.'

Such was the importance of the Cape Town Congress among evangelical Anglicans that it was celebrated in a worship service in All Souls Church, Langham Place, London. During the service, broadcast on BBC Radio, Rev Hugh Palmer reminded the congregation that theologian and writer, John Stott, who served All Souls Church as both Rector and Rector Emeritus for over 50 years, was closely involved in the first Lausanne Congress. Hugh Palmer explained that John Stott was 'largely responsible for drawing up the summary statement – the Lausanne Covenant – which ever since has stood as a defining statement for many Christians of our commitment and responsibilities to our world, and God's gospel purposes and love for it... John Stott's ministry and influence has stretched far beyond the walls of All Souls as he sought to build up the church, particularly in developing countries, through literature, scholarships and encouraging good, faithful preaching of the Word of God. These ministries have now been consolidated into the Langham Partnership International and taken forward under the leadership of the Revd Dr Chris Wright. Chris is also the Chair of the Theological Advisors to the Lausanne Movement.'[2]

The Cape Town Congress considered what it believed to be the critical issues of our time. Prominent issues included poverty and wealth; reconciliation; social justice; global warming; women's leadership; homosexuality; the 'oral' Bible; and spiritual warfare – as they all relate to the future of the Church and world evangelization. According to the Cape Town 2010 website, the purpose of this great gathering of Christian leaders was to 'examine the world and our culture to discern where the Church should invest its efforts and energies to most effectively respond to Christ's call to take the gospel into all the world and make disciples of all nations... lives changed for all eternity, broken families mended, physical and emotional hurts healed, communities transformed.'[3]

First Lausanne Congress (1974)

Billy Graham convened the International Congress on World Evangelism in Lausanne, Switzerland, in July 1974. The Congress was largely American planned, led and financed, and was sponsored by the magazine *Christianity Today*, with a large amount of support from the Billy Graham Evangelistic Association (BGEA). Lausanne I was a unique gathering, for never before had so many Christians from across the world met together in one place. It was indeed a global ground-breaking event and *Time* magazine called it 'possibly the widest-ranging meeting of Christians ever held'.[4]

In his opening address, Billy Graham boldly declared: 'I believe this could be one of the most significant gatherings not only in this century but in the history of the Christian Church… never before have so many representatives of so many evangelical Christian churches in so many nations and from so many tribal and language groups gathered to worship and pray and plan together for world evangelization.'[5] He concluded with the exhortation, 'We are gathered together to hear His voice.' Alongside Billy Graham were John Stott, Francis Schaeffer, Malcolm Muggeridge (who later converted to Roman Catholicism), Ralph D Winter and other prominent church leaders, including Rene Padilla and Samuel Escobar, the Latin American theologians who encouraged the Lausanne Movement to champion the cause of social justice. What started in Lausanne has ignited a Movement that is spread across the globe, serving thousands of churches and hundreds of the world's missionary organisations.

New Evangelicalism and Fuller Theological Seminary

Here we need to recognise the influence of the 'new evangelicals' on the Lausanne Movement. The ideas of the new evangelicals developed in the 1940s and 50s as a number of prominent Christian leaders, discontented with the doctrines and conduct of traditional evangelicalism, sought for a more liberal, accommodating form of evangelical Christianity. The new evangelicals saw traditional evangelicals, who they disparagingly referred to as 'fundamentalists', as harsh separatists who were unyielding in their faith and therefore divisive of Christian unity.

New evangelicals wanted a more loving faith that did not practise separation from unsound doctrine. The resulting 'new evangelicalism' (their own term) was a compromise; it demanded a 'tolerance' that avoided criticism of doctrinal error or the denouncing of false teaching. It was profoundly ecumenical in outlook, ready to form spiritual alliances with all shades of doctrine. Indeed, doctrine was regarded as not really important, especially when it caused controversy and division.

A vital step in promoting the ideas of new evangelicalism was the founding of the magazine *Christianity Today*. The young evangelist Billy Graham, with the support of his father-in-law, Nelson Bell, proposed the need for a publication that would 'plant the evangelical flag in the middle of the road, taking a conservative theological position but a definite liberal approach to social problems. It would combine the best in liberalism and the best in fundamentalism without compromising theologically.'[6] The magazine proved to be invaluable in promoting the crusades of the Billy Graham Evangelistic Association. Professor Carl Henry was editor when *Christianity Today* was first published in the fall of 1956.

The theological leaders of the new evangelicals were Dr Harold Ockenga and Carl Henry, both of whom played a key role in founding Fuller Theological Seminary, which became the new evangelicals' academic powerhouse in those early days. The term 'new evangelical' was probably coined by Ockenga, one of the most influential evangelical leaders of the time. As well as pastor of a Congregational church in Boston, USA, he was founder of the National Association of Evangelicals, a director of the Billy Graham Evangelistic Association, and chairman of *Christianity Today*, the flagship journal of the new evangelical movement. Ockenga described the philosophy of new evangelicalism in these words: 'The ringing call for a repudiation of separatism, and the summons to social involvement, received a hearty response from many evangelicals... We had no intention of launching a movement, but found that the emphasis attracted widespread support and exercised great influence. Neo-evangelicalism differed from modernism in its acceptance of the supernatural and its emphasis on the fundamental doctrines of Scripture... It differed from fundamentalism in its repudiation of separatism and its determination to engage itself in the theological dialogue of the day. It had a new emphasis upon the application of the gospel to the sociological, political and economic areas of life.'[7]

During the 1950s and 60s, Fuller Theological Seminary helped to further define new evangelicalism. By the middle of the 1960s the Seminary was firmly in the hands of scholars who were clearly and openly opposed to the doctrine of biblical inerrancy. In *The Battle for the Bible* (1976), Harold Lindsell, who served as a professor and vice-president of Fuller, wrote: 'In or about 1962 it became apparent that there were some who no longer believed in the inerrancy of the Bible, among both the faculty and the board members. One of the key board members, who was later to become chairman and whose wealth helped to underwrite the annual operating budget, was C Davis Weyerhaeuser... He was clear in his own conviction that the Bible had errors in it. Nor did he hesitate to make his position plain.'[8] In 1965 Fuller's School of Psychology was established to run alongside its School of Theology. The new School played a pivotal role in integrating humanistic theories of psychology and psychotherapy with the Christian faith, and fitted perfectly into Fuller's vision of a social gospel.

In 1967, Daniel Fuller, Dean of the Seminary, delivered a paper before the Evangelical Theological Society wherein he laid the groundwork for what may be called a doctrine of partial inspiration of Scripture.[9] He argued that there are two kinds of Scripture—revelational Scripture that is wholly without error and non-revelational Scripture that is not.[10] By the end of the 1960s, 'limited inerrancy' was the dominant view of the Seminary. An article in *Sword and Trowel* by Dr John Whitcomb, Professor of Theology at Grace Theological Seminary, defined the new evangelicalism 'as an attitude or mentality on the part of evangelicals to compromise – to some extent – the doctrines of Holy Scripture in order to be accepted by professing Christians outside the evangelical community. In other words, new evangelicalism begins with the heart.'[11]

Traditional evangelicals saw the new evangelicalism as a movement born of compromise. Pastor William Ashbrook wrote in the *Central Bible Quarterly* (1959) that this 'neutralism' (his term for new evangelicalism) 'is a position difficult to maintain in any age, but in a day like ours when the battle is pitched between Christ and anti-Christ it is an impossible position. In the sphere of things moral and spiritual a man must be either right or wrong. The showdown will come in realms of black or white, not in the fog of immaterial grey. There is no middle ground on which the neutralist can complacently stand for long... He is bound to wind up in one camp or other and in a day when God is judging compromise in no uncertain terms, he is very likely to wind up in the wrong camp. There can be no middle ground for Bible-believing Christians.'[12]

Although the word 'new' in the term 'new evangelical' was dispensed with a long time ago, the spirit and the beliefs of new evangelicalism are alive and well in our day. Modern new evangelicals, who now refer to themselves simply as 'evangelicals', exhibit some or all of the following characteristics. First, they have a low view of Scripture. Many interpret the first chapters of Genesis in a way that permits the doctrine of theistic evolution. Indeed, theistic evolution is virtually an article of faith for Anglican evangelicals. Second, they compromise on the biblical command to separate from false doctrine. It follows that they are ecumenical in outlook, eager to form spiritual alliances with all who profess to be Christian, whatever their beliefs. Third, they are reluctant to be separate from the ways of the world. Consequently worldly music forms part of their worship; and in the academic arena they strive for intellectual respectability in the hope of being accepted by the world. Fourth, they add a social component to the Gospel of salvation.

Fuller's influence on Lausanne

In the early 1970s Fuller Seminary changed its doctrinal statement to more accurately reflect the position held by members of its faculty. The original statement that Scripture is 'free from all error in the whole and in the part' was replaced by a more general statement: 'The Bible is infallible in those matters relating to faith and practice.' This new position left room for those who believe the Bible errs in matters of science and history. Moreover, the idea of the partial inspiration of Scripture, promoted by Daniel Fuller, presented a major dilemma for Bible interpretation, as Dr John Whitcomb points out in an article in *Sword and Trowel*: 'Obviously what was needed was a new edition of the Bible with only the inerrant portions in red and the rest in black, so that we would know what to quote, memorise and preach from. The absurdity of the new position is apparent, for who is going to tell us which portions of the Bible are really inerrant or truly revelatory, and which are not?'[13]

The position went from bad to worse when Dr Paul King Jewett, Fuller's professor of systematic theology, argued in his book, *Man as Male and Female* (1975), that the apostle Paul erred in the matter of a wife's submission to her husband. The apostle was simply wrong, said Jewett, for his teaching was merely a reflection of rabbinic thinking. John Whitcomb says that Jewett's book presented views which threatened to destroy the Bible entirely, regarding it as some culturally-conditioned ancient document that lacked authoritative control over our thinking today. 'Fuller Seminary was by now deteriorating so rapidly as to lose credibility even among many new evangelicals.'[14] Worse was to follow when Fuller's philosopher of religion, Jack Rogers, launched an even more formidable scholarly attack on inerrancy. In *The Authority and Interpretation of the Bible* (1979), he asserted that inerrancy 'had not been the teaching, or even the view, of those such as Augustine and Calvin whom evangelicals typically cited as great champions of the historic faith'.[15]

A further disaster struck Fuller Seminary in the early 1980s. John Whitcomb describes the new disaster as Fuller's 'flirtation with an extreme form of charismatic, experience-orientated subjectivism and mysticism. This entered the seminary through one of its professors, Peter Wagner, who recruited the proven false "prophet", John Wimber, presumably to help fill the vacuum left when faith in God's inerrant Word departed... For several years the subjectivism and mysticism of Wagner and Wimber began to permeate the theological atmosphere at Fuller Seminary, official courses being offered, with healings and exorcisms of demons being performed regularly. Students whose anchor was not in an inerrant Bible proved highly vulnerable.' As near chaos ruled in the classroom, seminary president David Hubbard 'expressed his judgement that the charismatic courses were not good for the Fuller image, and they were cancelled.'[16]

There is no doubt that the flawed theological ideas of Fuller Seminary, over the years, have been a major driving force behind the Lausanne Movement. At the first Congress in 1974, Lausanne leaders, with the help of Fuller's School of World Mission, set out to illustrate the immensity of the task of world evangelism through an ambitious data collection exercise. The objective of Fuller was to focus on 'unreached people groups', a new concept to the mission world.

One of the most important plenary sessions in 1974 was led by Donald McGavran, father of the church growth movement and founder of Fuller's School of World Mission. His book, *Bridges of God* (1954), originally titled, 'How Peoples Become Christian', promoted the idea of a 'people's movement' to Christ. He claimed that for a 'people's movement' to succeed the Gospel needed to be contextualised for each culture. In McGavran's mind, the focus of the Church should not be to save individuals, although that is not to be forgotten, but to redeem cultures by 'redemptive analogies'. He argued that 'extraction evangelism', that is, for one person to be saved out of the context of his sociological unit is a setback to global evangelization.[17] In his book, *Understanding Church Growth* (1970), McGavran set out the 'theological understandings, a wealth of empirical research, sociological principles and spiritual insights, which come together to develop a paradigm for a worldwide strategy for evangelism and church growth'.[18] He maintained that 'the greatest obstacles to conversion are social, not theological'.[19]

In a strategic paper for the 1974 Lausanne Congress, McGavran declared that 'the Christian Church has good news for the awakening masses – that God the Father Almighty is just and intends to have a just world. The revolutionary impact of this simple statement should be grasped. It affirms that the very structure of the universe favors the common man. It proclaims that God intends an order of society in which each man can and will receive justice. This meets the deepest needs of the proletariat... Their greatest need is neither handouts nor social action; but a religion which gives them bedrock on which to stand as they battle for justice'. He continued: 'The third mode of church growth is *the people movement to Christ*. In this, chains of families, all within the same segment of populations (the same caste, tribe, or culture unit) become Christians... *World evangelism should constantly be praying for and planning for family movements and people movements to Christ* [his italics].'[20]

In another plenary session, Fuller's Professor Ralph Winter gave a talk entitled, 'The Highest Priority: Cross-Cultural Evangelism'. Using statistics and graphs to support his case, he claimed that there were 2.5 billion people who could not hear the Gospel in their own languages and cultural setting. He concluded that a special kind of 'cross-cultural' evangelism is needed to take the Gospel to 'unreached people groups'. He said: 'I realise now that Christian unity cannot be healthy if it infringes on Christian liberty... I believe that there must be such a thing as healthy diversity in human society and in the Christian world Church.' His plea for culturally sensitive evangelism had a large impact on Lausanne's strategy for world evangelism.[21]

The Lausanne Covenant

The historic Lausanne Covenant was the major achievement of the first Congress; it was agreed upon by 2,700 people from 150 nations from virtually all branches of the Christian Church in the space of ten days. The Covenant, which is still used across the world, affirms that 'God is both the Creator and the Judge of all men. We therefore should share his concern for justice and reconciliation throughout human society and for the liberation of men from every kind of oppression... We express penitence both for our neglect and for having sometimes regarded evangelism and social concern as mutually exclusive.' The Covenant declares that 'the message of salvation implies also a message of judgment upon every form of alienation, oppression and discrimination, and we should not be afraid to denounce evil and injustice wherever they exist.'[22]

According to *Christianity Today*: 'In the end, the Lausanne Covenant spoke to the moment, expressing a common mission that most delegates could enthusiastically endorse; and it spoke to the future, providing a framework that evangelical groups could use as their basic statement. Lausanne was a defining moment in global evangelicalism. Billy Graham was the indispensable convener, but John Stott was the indispensable uniter.'[23] Many evangelical Christians regard the Covenant to be one of the most important documents in recent Church history, for they claim that it has brought together Christians from across the theological spectrum, challenging all to work together to make Jesus Christ known throughout the world. The Covenant has been translated into more than 20 languages, and adopted by thousands of churches and para-church agencies as their basis of operations and cooperation.

The term 'evangelization'

The first Lausanne Congress adopted the term *evangelization*, in place of the more traditional term *evangelism*. The significance of *evangelization* is that it calls for a renewed mission to the world with a more holistic approach to evangelism. Rather than just preaching the Gospel of salvation from sin and new life in Christ, living a life of obedience to God's commandments, and daily striving for holiness, *evangelization* encouraged Christians to commit themselves to the cause of social justice, with a special interest in the needs of the poor and oppressed.

The commitment to *evangelization* meant that the Lausanne Congress was able to affirm that 'evangelism and socio-political involvement are both part of our Christian duty'.[24]

Here we should note that the term *evangelization* was popularised in the encyclical of Pope Paul VI entitled *Evangelization in the Modern World* (1975). According to the encyclical, evangelization in its totality 'consists in the implantation of the Church, which does not exist without the driving force which is the sacramental life culminating in the Eucharist.'[25] The Roman Catholic Church 'strives always to insert the Christian struggle for liberation into the universal plan of salvation which she herself proclaims... The necessity of ensuring fundamental human rights cannot be separated from this just liberation which is bound up with evangelization and which endeavours to secure structures safeguarding human freedoms.'[26] But how many Protestant evangelicals understand that the term *evangelization* is widely used by the Church of Rome to explain what it regards as the real meaning of the Gospel?

In 1990 Pope John Paul II, in his encyclical *Mission of the Redeemer*, again emphasised the Roman Catholic teaching about evangelization.[27] He said that as the third millennium drew near there was a new consensus among peoples about these values, 'the rejection of violence and war; respect for the human person and for human rights; the desire for freedom, justice and brotherhood; the surmounting of different forms of racism and nationalism; the affirmation of the dignity and role of women. Christian hope sustains us in committing ourselves fully to the new evangelization and to the worldwide mission...'[28] So in the eyes of the Vatican evangelization involves the liberation of men, social action, human rights and the promotion of fraternal love. While the average Christian probably sees little difference between *evangelism* and *evangelization*, the reality is that they are fundamentally different ways of understanding and preaching the Gospel – the first is biblical, while the second is centred on the 'Eucharistic Christ', Mother Church and an infallible Pope, and aims, like Lausanne to transform cultures.

The great commission of the Christian Church is to 'go into all the world and preach the gospel to every creature' (Mark 16.15). *Evangelism* involves preaching the Gospel of salvation from sin in order that souls might be saved. The essential message is 'Christ Jesus came into the world to save sinners' (1 Timothy 1.15). All true Christians know that they cannot earn salvation. 'For by grace you have been saved through faith, and that not of yourselves; it is a gift of God, not of works, lest anyone should boast' (Ephesians 2.8-9). *Evangelization*, on the other hand, means the saving of whole nations or 'people groups' spiritually and temporally through political and social action. It appears that the Lausanne view of evangelization, which combines social and political action with the message of salvation, is remarkably similar to the Vatican version of evangelization, which strives for fundamental human rights and structures that safeguard human freedoms.

Billy Graham, honorary chairman of the Lausanne Committee for World Evangelization, boldly declared: 'Evangelism has taken on a new meaning. It is a time of great opportunity, but also a time of great responsibility. We are stewards of our Christian heritage. We must evangelize at all costs while there is yet time. World problems of poverty, overpopulation and the threat of nuclear war mount by the hour. The world is in desperate need of the gospel, now!' And so the Lausanne Congress introduced a new way of evangelism that placed the message of personal salvation from sin alongside the message of social justice. It was clear from the beginning that the new method – by works rather than by grace through faith – was committed to combining evangelism with radical social action. This new way had little time for the niceties of sound doctrine grounded on biblical truth.

Church Growth Theory

In 1977 the Lausanne Theology and Education Group held a seminar on church growth theory, hosted by Fuller Seminary, with John Stott acting as moderator. This was the first consultation to be held under Lausanne's sponsorship since the 1974 Congress.[29] Five faculty members of Fuller's School of World Mission prepared papers for the meeting, including Donald McGavran, Ralph Winter and Peter Wagner. In addition, 12 of the 27 consultants were from Fuller Seminary; even Seminary president Daniel Fuller was part of the consultation.

This gathering spoke volumes about the theological stance of Lausanne. It was now abundantly clear that Fuller Seminary, with its flawed view of Scripture, its theological compromise and charismatic

11

confusion, was the driving force behind the Lausanne Movement. It was also clear that theologian John Stott, the architect of Lausanne, was perfectly comfortable working hand in hand with the new evangelical agenda of Fuller Seminary.

Lausanne II in Manila (1989)

The Second Lausanne Congress, in Manila in 1989, was attended by representatives from 173 countries. A feature of the Congress was a new openness to charismatic influences. Peter Wagner explains: 'In dramatic contrast to Lausanne I, held in Switzerland in 1974, Lausanne II embraced leaders of the Pentecostal/charismatic movements at all levels from the Lausanne Committee itself through the plenary sessions and workshops to the thousands of participants who regularly worshiped with raised hands. Remarkably, the three most attended workshop tracks (of 48 offered) were on the Holy Spirit, spiritual warfare and prayer.'[30] Charismatic pastor Jack Hayford played a prominent role in plenary sessions, which followed a contemporary style of worship. So-called 'power evangelism' was promoted by the Fuller tandem, Peter Wagner and John Wimber.

A prominent presence at Manila was Dr Eugene Stockwell, a leader of the ecumenical World Council of Churches. Other official observers and special guests came from the Vatican, the Russian Orthodox Church and the Greek Orthodox Church. The Congress felt the need to publicly repent of their narrow view of the Gospel. 'The narrowness of our concerns and vision has often kept us from proclaiming the lordship of Jesus Christ over all of life, private and public, local and global.'[31] The Manila Manifesto (drafted by John Stott) stated that women 'must be given opportunities to exercise their gifts', and deplored failures in Christian consistency – including sexual discrimination – affirming that 'cooperation in evangelism is indispensable' with 'both sexes working together'. The Congress gave birth to more than 300 strategic partnerships in world evangelization.

The Manifesto affirmed the need for cooperation in evangelism. 'Evangelical attitudes to the Roman Catholic and Orthodox Churches differ widely. Some evangelicals are praying, talking, studying Scripture and working with these churches. Others are strongly opposed to any form of dialogue or cooperation with them. All are aware that serious theological differences between us remain. Where appropriate, and so long as biblical truth is not compromised, cooperation may be possible in such areas as Bible translation, the study of contemporary theological and ethical issues, social work and political action. We wish to make it clear, however, that common evangelism demands a common commitment to the biblical gospel.'[32]

This ambiguous statement, typical of new evangelicalism, was designed to be all things to all men. It sought to placate those who still followed the doctrines of the Reformation, while at the same time offering encouragement to those of an ecumenical bent who were keen to work alongside the Roman Catholic Church. But the Manifesto did not make clear how in practice there could be 'common evangelism' without a common understanding of the biblical Gospel. It was not at all clear whether or not Lausanne accepted the Gospel of the Roman Catholic Church as a biblical Gospel. Neither was the position of Lausanne's leadership with regard to the doctrines of the Reformation made clear.

Amsterdam 2000 Conference

In 2000 the Billy Graham Association convened the Amsterdam Conference, which brought together 10,000 evangelists from across the world, many of them from Third World nations. Prominent speakers included Luis Palau, JI Packer, John Stott, Ravi Zacharias, and Archbishop George Carey. Rev Nicky Gumbel, well known as the promoter of the Alpha course (discussed in chapter 8), received a personal invitation from Billy Graham to run a workshop. 'Your experience and expertise as a leader will be a great asset to the conference, and participants will gain invaluable knowledge and insight from the content of the workshop.'[33]

As part of its worldwide scope, the nine-day event dealt with a series of cutting-edge, socially relevant topics. The Amsterdam Declaration addressed a variety of issues, including social responsibility and evangelism. Those signing the Declaration affirmed the need 'to stay involved personally in grass-roots evangelism so that our presentations of the biblical gospel are fully relevant and contextualized... When our evangelism is linked with concern to alleviate poverty, uphold justice, oppose abuses of secular and economic power, stand against racism, and advance responsible stewardship of the global environment, it reflects the compassion of Christ and may gain an acceptance it would not otherwise receive. We pledge ourselves to follow the way of justice in our family and social life, and to keep personal, social, and environmental values in view as we evangelize.'[34]

Billy Graham asked Paul Eshleman, who was running the Jesus Film project, to gather together 600 missionary leaders from across the world to deal with the issue of unreached people groups. During group discussions, Marcus Vegh of Progressive Vision asked missionary leader Avery Willis, 'How do you make disciples of oral learners?' The question made a strong impression on Willis: 'I heard his voice as if it were the voice of God. I am not sure why it hit me so hard. While serving as Senior Vice-President for Overseas Operations with the International Mission Board of Southern Baptists I had helped lead our 5,000 missionaries to focus on reaching the unreached. I was aware of oral learners and Chronological Bible Storying but never considered they were my responsibility. Now I heard God telling me it was... The goal was to help evangelize and make disciples, and to begin to nurture indigenous church planting movements.'[35]

As a consequence of Amsterdam 2000 plans were made to explore oral methods of communicating the Gospel.[36] The issue of orality (or storytelling the Gospel) was now firmly on the Lausanne agenda, as an increasing number of mission groups began to think about how to effectively communicate the Gospel among so-called 'oral people' groups. Amsterdam 2000 was a significant step towards the creation of the International Orality Network discussed in chapter 7.

This book tells the tragic story of theological compromise. In the following chapters we shall see that theological compromise never stands still, but leads to further compromise. We shall also see that theological compromise has consequences, for it undermines the witness of the Church as the pillar and foundation of truth. Those who are willing to accept a little compromise as a price worth paying for the sake of unity, and to avoid theological conflict, are deluding themselves. The story of the Lausanne Movement, founded by Billy Graham and John Stott, illustrates these two principles.

(Endnotes)

1 The Lausanne Movement website, 'Why Cape Town 2010? A Case-Statement for the Third Lausanne Congress' by Doug Birdsall, Executive Chair, http://www.lausanne.org/en/gatherings/cape-town-2010/why-cape-town-2010.html

2 Sunday Worship from All Souls, Langham Place, London. Last broadcast on Sun, 17 Oct 2010, 08:10 on BBC Radio 4.

3 Cape Town 2010 website, http://www.lausanne.org/cape-town-2010/about.html

4 Lausanne Movement History Video, http://www.youtube.com/watch?v=mZcQGYIWhR8&feature=related

5 Lausanne Movement History Video, http://www.youtube.com/watch?v=mZcQGYIWhR8&feature=related

6 Letter from Billy Graham to Harold Lindsell, cited from *Reforming Fundamentalism – Fuller Seminary and the New Evangelicalism* by George M Marsden, William B Eerdmans, paperback edition 1995, p158

7 Harold Lindsell, *The Battle for the Bible*, Zondervan Publishing House, 1976, Foreword written by Dr Harold Ockenga

8 Ibid. p108

9 Website of Evangelical Reformed Fellowship, 'The Necessary Consonance of the Doctrines of Scripture: Inspiration, Inerrancy, and Authority' by Steve Curtis

10 *The Battle for the Bible*, p113

11 John Whitcomb, 'The new evangelicals burst into view', *Sword and Trowel*, 1987, No. 3, p34

12 William A Ashbrook, *The New Evangelism - The New Neutralism*, in Central Bible Quarterly, Summer 1959

13 John Whitcomb, 'The hastening disaster', *Sword and Trowel*, 1988, No. 1, p4

14 Ibid. p4

15 George M Marsden, *Reforming Fundamentalism – Fuller Seminary and the New Evangelicalism*, Eerdmans Publishing, 1987, p285

16 John Whitcomb, *Sword and Trowel*, 1988, No. 1, p5

17 Seek God website, The Fuller Theological Think Tank, Donald McGavran, http://www.seekgod.ca/fuller2.htm#mcgavran

18 Church Education Trust website, Comments on Chapter 2, 'The Church Growth Movement'. www.churcheducationtrust.com/index.html?id=86

19 Cited from, 'Concerns About the Church Growth Movement' by Wayne D. Schoch, [A paper presented at the Lake Superior Pastoral Conference on April 27, 1993.]

20 Paper for Lausanne Congress, 1974, by Donald A McGavran, entitled 'The Dimensions of World Evangelism', http://www.lausanne.org/docs/lau1docs/0094.pdf

21 Paper for Lausanne Congress, 1974, by Ralph D Winter, entitled 'The Highest Priority: Cross-cultural Evangelism', http://www.lausanne.org/docs/lau1docs/0226.pdf

22 Lausanne Covenant, Christian Social Responsibility, http://www.lausanne.org/covenant

23 *Christianity Today*, 27 July 2011, (web only), 'John Stott Has Died, An architect of 20th-century evangelicalism shaped the faith of a generation' by Tim Stafford

24 The Lausanne Movement website, Lausanne Covenant, Christian Social Responsibility, http://www.lausanne.org/en/documents/lausanne-covenant.html

25 Evangelii Nuntiandi, Apostolic Exhortation of His Holiness, Pope Paul VI, paragraph 28

26 Ibid. paragraphs 38 and 39

27 Redemptoris Missio, (On the Permanent Validity of the Church's Missionary Mandate), John Paul II, Encyclical promulgated on 7 December 1990

28 Ibid. paragraph 86

29 Lausanne Occasional Paper 1, Pasadena Consultation - Homogeneous Unit Principle, 1978, Lausanne Committee for World Evangelization

30 Peter C Wagner, *Wrestling With Dark Angels: Toward a Deeper Understanding of the Supernatural Forces in Spiritual Warfare*, Monarch Books, 1990, p6, cited from the Seeking God website, http://www.seekgod.ca/darkangels.htm

31 The Lausanne Movement website, The Manila Manifesto, 1989, affirmation 4, The Gospel and Social Responsibility, http://www.lausanne.org/all-documents/manila-manifesto. html

32 Ibid. The Manila Manifesto, 1989, affirmation 9, Cooperating in Evangelism

33 Billy Graham Invites Alpha, Alpha News Online, No. 3, March-July 2000

34 'The Amsterdam Declaration, A Charter for evangelism in the 21st century', *Christianity Today*, August 2000, (web only)

35 Avery T. Willis, Foreword to *Orality Breakouts*, published by International Orality Network, 2010, pp5-6, http://www.heartstories.info/sites/default/files/Foreword.pdf

36 The International Orality Network, History of ION, http://www.oralbible.com/about/ history

Chapter 2

Billy Graham – the ecumenical evangelist

One of the most important and far-reaching achievements of Billy Graham was to set up and nurture the Lausanne Movement. Widely regarded as the greatest evangelist of our age, it is claimed that he has preached to more people in live audiences than any other person in history (estimated in total to be over 210 million). His official biography states that since 1949 he has led hundreds of thousands of individuals to make personal decisions to live for Christ. *Christianity Today* has acknowledged the massive contribution of Graham to the evangelical cause. The article says it would be difficult to overestimate Billy Graham's importance in the last 50 years of evangelicalism, for he personally embodied most of the characteristics of resurgent evangelicalism; he also de-emphasised doctrinal and denominational differences that often divided Christians. 'For evangelicalism, Billy Graham has meant the reconstruction of a Christian fellowship transcending confessional lines—a grassroots ecumenism that regards denominational divisions as irrelevant rather than pernicious.'[1] Graham used his good reputation among evangelical Christians to set up, together with John Stott, the Lausanne Movement for the evangelization of the world.

Billy Graham has played a huge part in the ecumenical movement over five decades, and so it's no surprise that the roots of Lausanne are deeply grounded in ecumenism. In an interview with the *Bookstore Journal*, Graham said that he began to realise in the 1950s 'that there were Christians everywhere. They might be called modernists, Catholics, or whatever, but they were Christians'.[2] He believed that for evangelicals to reach a wider audience it was necessary to accept a few doctrinal compromises. The argument was that as long as there was agreement over the essentials of the Gospel other matters were of secondary importance.

London Crusade (1954)

It was the Greater London Crusade of 1954 that launched Billy Graham's ministry as an international evangelist. The 12-week crusade, sponsored by the British Evangelical Alliance, was the longest that he had yet attempted and received a great deal of media attention. Meetings in the Harringay Arena, which seated 12,000, were packed out every night, with hundreds coming forward to accept Christ. In addition to the nightly Harringay meetings there were a number of special events, including rallies in Hyde Park, Trafalgar Square and elsewhere. The final event in Wembley Stadium was attended by a massive crowd of 120,000. The reputation of Billy Graham as a world evangelist was well and truly established.

New York City Crusade (1957)

The New York City Crusade of 1957 marked a turning point in Graham's career. In the early 1950s it was widely believed that the evangelist's ministry was firmly based in his fundamentalist roots. And so in 1950 a committee of 'fundamentalist' Christians, acting on behalf of several hundred ministers, invited the Billy Graham Evangelistic Association to hold a campaign in New York. In his letter to the committee, Graham said that he was only willing to go forward if 'the Committee unanimously endorse the program of an ecumenical spirit to be exhibited throughout the campaign. I am willing that we should go forward with the present Committee, if in all our actions we shall present an ecumenical spirit of love toward those of all stripes. I have never been, nor will I ever be in favour of a modernist being on the committee'.[3] After further discussions it became clear that Graham was unable to work with the fundamentalist ministers. He therefore rejected their invitation.

In 1955 Graham received an invitation from the liberal Protestant Council of the City of New York, an affiliate of the National Council of Churches, to hold an evangelistic campaign in the city. It soon became apparent that Graham was at ease working with the Council, an organisation that included out-and-out modernists. Indeed, his position had moved to such an extent that he reneged on his vow never to have a modernist on the campaign committee, for the planning committee of the New York crusade was composed of about 120 modernists/liberals and about 20 fundamentalists.[4]

Graham's ecumenical vision was so wide that he was even willing to work with the 'positive thinking' messages of Norman Vincent Peale. Peale's so-called 'practical Christianity' was simply a euphemism for his therapeutic, mystical message driven by the 'felt needs' of his audience. According to his critics, 'It was a kind of shadow religion, a distorted and dangerous adaptation of the real thing. Peale's cosmic and transcendental concept of divinity was viewed as blasphemous because it seemed to reduce God to human proportions and to make God the servant of humanity'.[5] Despite serious concerns that Peale's message of 'positive thinking' was inconsistent with biblical truth, he was a member of Graham's New York planning committee.

Graham agreed with his modernist sponsors that new converts would be sent back to their local churches, no matter how liberal they were.[6] Several newspapers reported the evangelist as saying of those who responded to his appeal: 'We'll send them to their own churches – Roman Catholic, Protestant or Jewish... the rest is up to God'.[7]

The New York City Crusade, which commenced on 16 May 1957 and ran for 16 weeks with 100 meetings, was undoubtedly a massive success. Most meetings were held in Madison Square Gardens, which seated around 20,000. A special mid-campaign event in Yankee Stadium drew the largest crowd in the Stadium's history. The final meeting of the crusade in Time Square was attended by a crowd estimated to be 120,000. Total attendance for the whole campaign was over two million people with 56,000 'decisions' for Christ. A survey by *Life* magazine, however, revealed that four-fifths of the 'decisions' were made by people who were already church members. Nevertheless, Norman Vincent Peale was particularly pleased as his church received the largest number of new converts.[8]

The significance of the New York Crusade is that it made public the split between Graham and his fundamentalist roots. According to *Christianity Today*: 'Graham decided to take on the fundamentalists in the spring of 1957, warning the National Association of Evangelicals at their annual meeting that took place in upstate New York that they "could slip into extreme ultra-fundamentalism". But fundamentalist leaders like Bob Jones Sr said Graham had "sold out to the modernists" by inviting all churches to participate in his services.'[9]

John R Rice, a Baptist evangelist, was one of Graham's last fundamentalist supporters. Rice was the founding editor of *The Sword of the Lord*, a bi-weekly Baptist newspaper, and Graham was a member of the board. Rice had been a great supporter of Graham's early ministry, but he was now disillusioned and wrote in *The Sword*: 'Dr Graham is one of the spokesmen, and perhaps the principal spark plug, of a great drift away from strict Bible fundamentalism and strict defence of the faith.'[10]

The booklet, 'Should Fundamentalists Support the Billy Graham Crusades' (1957), written by Dr Ernest Pickering and published by the Independent Fundamental Churches of America, was a reasoned summary of the fundamentalist position against Graham's ecumenical zeal. Pickering said that Graham had 'been caught in a web of unscriptural practices from which he now will find it difficult to break'.[11] He argued that by insisting that modernistic ministers and churches be included in his sponsoring organisations, Graham was referring new converts to liberal churches.[12] Pickering asserted: 'Billy Graham has openly repudiated fundamentalism and is a leader in the New Evangelical Movement.'[13]

Having rejected his fundamentalist roots, Graham announced that his 'inclusive policy' meant infiltrating rather than separating from those with doctrinal differences. He defended his position by claiming: 'The one badge of Christian discipleship is not orthodoxy, but love.'[14] As a consequence of this policy his future evangelical campaigns would work closely with modernists, liberals and Roman Catholics. In the future his ministry would deliver thousands of converts into the Church of Rome.

Los Angeles Crusade (1963)

Consistent with his commitment to the modernist cause, in 1963 Billy Graham chose a liberal Methodist bishop, Gerald Kennedy, to be the honorary chairman of his Los Angeles Crusade. The theological beliefs of Bishop Kennedy were stated in his Episcopal Address to the Methodist Church in 1964. He said: 'We rejoice in the growth of the ecumenical movement and in the development of the ecumenical spirit... We believe in and we support the World Council of Churches, the National Councils of Churches… We rejoice in the new spirit of ecumenical fellowship which comes out of the Second Vatican Council. We will go as far as our Roman Catholic brethren will allow in meeting together for mutual consultation and witness.'[15] This was the man chosen by Graham to represent the public image of his campaign. The split between Billy Graham and fundamentalists that occurred in New York had clearly grown into a chasm.

Billy Graham's relationship with the Roman Catholic Church

During the Boston Crusade in 1964, Graham requested a meeting with Cardinal Richard Cushing, Archbishop of Boston. At their meeting the Cardinal is reported as saying to Graham: 'Well, I'm a Catholic, but I'm for you. No Catholic can listen to you without becoming a better Catholic. You preach Catholic as well as Protestant doctrine.' Graham said that his preaching was much closer to the theology of the Roman Catholic Church than it was to some of those he considered to be far-out Protestants. His comfortable working relationship with Catholics would continue throughout the rest of his ministry.[16]

In Milwaukee in 1973 Graham preached the funeral sermon for a close friend in the Catholic Cathedral. Several bishops and archbishops participated in the service and Graham said: 'As I sat there going through the funeral Mass that was a very beautiful thing and certainly straight and clear in the gospel I believe, there was a wonderful little priest that would tell me when to stand and when to kneel and what to do…'[17] Graham's comments about the beauty of the Mass say a great deal about his high view of the Church of Rome.

Graham frequently praised the Pope and even stated that the Mass is scriptural.[18] In an article in 1980 Graham wrote that 'Pope John Paul II has emerged as the greatest religious leader of the modern world, and one of the greatest moral and spiritual leaders of the century.'[19]

In 1988 Graham was quoted in *U.S. News & World Report*: 'World travel and getting to know clergy of all denominations has helped mold me into an ecumenical being. We're separated by theology and, in some instances, culture and race, but all of that means nothing to me any more.'[20] Graham's Seattle-Tacoma Crusade in 1991 accepted Roman Catholic priests as counsellors as long as they went through the training. And people who made a decision for Christ were referred to Roman Catholic churches if they indicated they were Catholic in a questionnaire.[21]

In 1996 Graham wrote an editorial for *Christianity Today*: 'Who could have envisioned the almost explosive growth of evangelicals during the last four decades? Who could have foreseen the impact this magazine would have, not only in evangelical circles but far beyond? God alone must get the credit... During our recent evangelistic crusade in Minneapolis we witnessed one of the largest responses to the gospel message we have ever seen. I am convinced the main reason was prayer, as believers from almost every denomination (including Roman Catholics) sought the face of God in intercession for their area.'[22]

Larry King, the popular American television chat show host, interviewed Billy Graham on his programme in January 1997 and asked him if he was comfortable with the Vatican. Graham replied that he was very comfortable with the Vatican. He said: 'I have been to see the Pope several times. In fact, the night – the day that he was inaugurated, made Pope, I was preaching in his cathedral in Krakow. I was his guest... [and] when he was over here... in Columbia, South Carolina... he invited me on the platform to speak with him. I would give one talk, and he would give the other.'[23]

In an interview with Sir David Frost in May 1997, Billy Graham made his ecumenical position absolutely clear: 'I feel I belong to all the churches. I'm equally at home in an Anglican or Baptist or a Brethren assembly or a Roman Catholic Church... Today we have almost 100 percent Catholic support in this country. That was not true twenty years ago. And the bishops and archbishops and the Pope are our friends.'[24]

Autobiography of Billy Graham

In his autobiography, *Just As I Am* (1997), Graham goes to some length to convince the reader that he holds the Roman Catholic Church in high esteem. He says he was profoundly impressed with Mother Teresa. 'I was deeply touched not only by her work, but also by her humility and Christian love. She mentioned that she had held five dying people in her arms the night before and talked with them about God and His love as they were dying. When I asked her why she did what she did, she quietly pointed to the figure of Christ on the Cross hanging on her wall.'[25]

Graham describes a brief visit to the Vatican in 1981. 'Our first reaction was that the magnificence of the public areas of the Vatican was surpassed, if anything, by that of the private areas… As I was ushered into his quarters, Pope John Paul II greeted me, and we shook hands warmly. I found him extremely cordial and very interested in our ministry, especially in his homeland. After only a few minutes, I felt as if we had known each other for many years.'[26]

After reassuring Roman Catholic officials that he was not anti-Catholic, Poland's Catholic episcopate supported his planned visit to Poland and invited him to preach in four of the country's major cathedrals. Graham writes: 'I would not have done or said anything that might be taken as anti-Catholic. During the month of October, we went to six major cities, proclaiming the Gospel from a variety of pulpits and platforms (including Roman Catholic, Baptist, Reformed and Lutheran) to many thousands of attentive listeners.'[27]

Graham was impressed with the religious devotion of Catholic Poland. 'We visited various shrines and churches, including in Czestochowa the shrine of the Black Madonna, Poland's most famous icon, dating back to 1382, which was housed in a basilica that was the most renowned Catholic shrine in central Europe. We were guests of the gracious abbot there. He invited me to come some year to preach at the annual pilgrimage, where upward of 1 million people would be present.'[28]

Billy Graham leaves the reader in no doubt that he regards Roman Catholics as fellow Christians. He goes out of his way to ingratiate himself with the Catholic hierarchy and stresses the point that he is not anti-Catholic, for he has so much in common with his many Catholic friends.

To rightly interpret the Lausanne Movement we need to understand Graham's devotion to the Roman Catholic Church, even finding the Mass a thing of beauty. He clearly has no major disagreement with the doctrines of the Catholic Church, and is perfectly happy to support its ministry. The question to ask is to what extent his close fellowship with Catholicism has influenced Lausanne?

Martyn Lloyd-Jones refused to endorse Graham

Doctor Martyn Lloyd-Jones, for three decades minister of Westminster Chapel in London and widely regarded as one of the foremost leaders among Reformed evangelical Christians in the UK, refused to endorse Billy Graham's crusades. Lloyd-Jones expressed his reservations in an interview with Carl Henry published in 1980. Asked why his church did not support the Billy Graham crusades, Lloyd-Jones replied, 'It seems to me that the campaign approach trusts ultimately in techniques rather than in the power of the Spirit.' Lloyd-Jones explained that Graham had invited him to chair the 1963 Congress on Evangelism. 'I said I'd make a bargain: if he would stop the general sponsorship of his campaigns—stop having liberals and Roman Catholics on the platform—and drop the invitation system, I would wholeheartedly support him and chair the congress… but he didn't accept these conditions.'[29]

Graham's shaky theology

Billy Graham never received any formal theological training, and, although his roots were in conservative Baptist theology, as his career developed it became apparent that he had a poor grasp of basic Christian doctrines. He became increasingly adept at putting to one side the doctrinal distinctives that had once defined him as a traditional evangelical Christian. In recognition of a life devoted to evangelism, the Southern Baptist Convention voted to commission a huge statue to honour Billy Graham. The statue was unveiled in June 2006 at the annual meeting of the Southern Baptist Convention, and while Baptist leaders applauded his evangelistic fervour and impassioned preaching style, they were noticeably silent regarding his theology, with good reason.[30]

The reason for doubts about his theology came mainly from frequent interviews that received wide coverage in the mass media. Asked whether Jews, Muslims, Buddhists, Hindus and other non-Christians, will go to heaven, the best Billy Graham could do was: 'Those are decisions only the Lord will make. It would be foolish for me to speculate about all that. I believe the love of God is absolute. He said he gave his Son for the whole world, and I think he loves everybody regardless of what label they have.'[31]

In 1982 Billy Graham was awarded the Templeton Prize for Progress in Religion. The Prize celebrates no particular faith tradition or notion of God, but rather the quest for progress in humanity's efforts to comprehend the many and diverse manifestations of the Divine.[32] Its focus is on ecumenical and New Age ventures that are regarded by Templeton as helping religions to make progress. Such was Graham's doctrinal vagueness that he was regarded as an ideal candidate for the Templeton award. And such was Graham's ecumenical spirit that he felt honoured to accept the award. Indeed, such is his celebrity status, and so much is he loved by the world, that he has also been awarded a 'star' on the Hollywood Walk of Fame.

In May 1997 Billy Graham was interviewed by Dr Robert Schuller, the most popular televangelist of the age and pastor of the Crystal Cathedral in Orange County, California. Schuller was a disciple of Norman Vincent Peale's 'positive thinking', and his populist self-help brand of preaching enabled him to build a mega-church. In his book, *Self-Esteem: The New Reformation* (1982), Schuller wrote: 'If the gospel of Jesus Christ can be proclaimed as a theology of self-esteem, imagine the health this could generate in society.'[33] He taught that salvation is to be delivered from poor self-esteem.

Yet Graham's ecumenical mindset and doctrinal vagueness meant that he was happy to be part of Schuller's self-help populist message. During the 'Hour of Power' TV show, Schuller asked Graham about his view of the future of Christianity. Graham responded: 'I think there's the Body of Christ. This comes from all the Christian groups around the world, outside the Christian groups. I think everybody that loves Christ, or knows Christ, whether they're conscious of it or not, they're members of the Body of Christ... And that's what God is doing today, He's calling people out of the world for His name, whether they come from the Muslim world, or the Buddhist world, or the Christian world or the non-believing world, they are members of the Body of Christ because they've been called by God. They may not even know the name of Jesus but they know in their hearts they need something that they don't have, and they turn to the only light that they have, and I think they are saved, and that they're going to be with us in heaven.'[34]

In the David Frost interview of May 1997, referred to above, Sir David produced a quote of Graham saying that his daughter Ann is a great Bible teacher among women. Frost then asked whether Graham was in favour of the ordination of women. Graham responded: 'It would be according to the circle I was in because I'm – I feel that I belong to all the churches. I'm equally at home in an Anglican or a Baptist church or a Brethren assembly or a Roman Catholic church. And I would have to say that I would identify with the customs and the culture and the theology of that particular church.'[35] This statement suggests that Graham has no clear theological understanding of the role of women in the Church. He openly declares that his vacillating position was based on the customs and culture of the particular church that he happened to be dealing with, and therefore was not based on Scripture. By avoiding a clear position he was able to be all things to all people; he succeeded in pleasing men rather than God.

What is clear from the above interviews is that Graham appears to place little importance upon doctrinal truth. In *A Prophet with Honor - The Billy Graham Story* (1992), William Martin included the following: 'Robert Ferm who spent a career putting the best possible face on Graham's actions and words [stated], "I have read the major theologians and his [theology] is in an entirely different category." Carl Henry admitted that "I keep my fingers crossed about the books Billy writes." Still another veteran colleague was more blunt: "Billy has never worked through his theology".'[36]

In his book, *Answers to Life's Problems* (1988), Graham writes that although faith in God is very, very important, 'God may choose to use an able psychiatrist to help you with some of the problems you are facing... Therefore, you should not feel that you are wrong in seeking the help of a psychiatrist or trained psychologist if that will help you deal with some deep-seated emotional problems. Seek one who will not discourage your faith in God. Your pastor can perhaps suggest a Christian psychiatrist in your area.'[37] Graham is saying that a believer with deep-seated emotional problems needs more than Christ can offer – so he needs a psychiatrist. Scripture says that Christ's divine power has given us all things that pertain to life and godliness (2 Peter 1.3). Christ is our great High Priest who is able to sympathise with our weaknesses. Therefore in our time of trouble we must draw near to the throne of grace that we might receive mercy and find grace to help in our time of need (Hebrews 4.15-16). In other words, Christ is sufficient and willing to supply all our needs, even our deep-seated emotional needs, according to his riches in glory. But Graham, it appears, does not believe in the sufficiency of Christ, and so he supports a psychotherapeutic approach that is based on the ideas of humanistic psychology. My book, *The Dark Side of Christian Counselling* (2009), deals with this issue in more detail.

In an interview on Fox News (January 2000), Tony Snow asked Graham, 'When you get to Heaven, who's going to speak first, you or God?' Graham responded that Jesus would either welcome him or may tell him that he is in the wrong place. Snow: 'You really worry that you may be told you're in the wrong place?' Graham: 'Yes, because I have not – I'm not a righteous man. People put me up on a pedestal that I don't belong [on] in my personal life. And they think that I'm better than I am. I'm not the good man that people think I am. Newspapers and magazines and television have made me out to be a saint. I'm not. I'm not a Mother Teresa. And I feel that very much.'[38] Graham was concerned that he was not righteous enough to deserve heaven, for he was not as righteous as Mother Teresa. This is a strange reply, for it suggests that Graham believes that his hope of heaven depends on his own righteousness. He even seems to think that the righteousness of Mother Teresa is good enough for heaven. Yet a true believer knows that his righteousness is as filthy rags in the sight of God (Isaiah 64.6). A true believer also knows that he has been justified, that is made right with God, by faith alone in the blood of Christ. He has the imputed righteousness of God and therefore there is no condemnation (Romans 5.1 and 8.1). He has been sealed with the Holy Spirit, he knows whom he has believed and his hope of heaven is certain, for Christ has promised, 'My sheep hear my voice, and I know them, and they follow me: And I give unto them eternal life; and they shall never perish, neither shall any man pluck them out of my hand' (John 10.27-28). Graham's theological confusion is such that on the one hand he seems to doubt his own salvation, but on the other hand he assures us that non-Christians are included in the body of Christ, 'and I think they are saved, and that they're going to be with us in heaven'.

In his book, *Billy Graham and Rome* (2009), David Cloud carefully documents Graham's relationship with Rome over the years. 'These are not isolated facts but exemplify Graham's philosophy and methodology through the years. For half a century Graham has turned inquirers over to Catholic churches, has accepted honorary degrees from Catholic schools, has flattered the popes with amazing accolades, and has visited

Pope John Paul II to seek his counsel. In the evangelical world, Billy Graham has no equal, nor does he have an equal in the building up of Roman Catholicism. More that any other man Billy Graham has paved the way for the widespread acceptance of a Catholic pope by Protestants and Baptists. His groundbreaking but unscriptural ecumenical evangelism has downplayed doctrine and exalted experiential religious unity.'[39]

The Billy Graham Evangelistic Association

The Billy Graham Evangelistic Association (BGEA) has spread the Billy Graham legend worldwide. The Association is now in the hands of Graham's fourth son Franklin, who has become an evangelist after the pattern of his famous father. But rather than evangelistic crusades, Franklin specialises in seeker-sensitive evangelistic festivals, which use rock bands to draw in the youthful crowds. These festivals are held in cities across the world.

A series of festivals across the United States and Canada are known as 'Rock the River'. Graham was very candid about his reason for making use of rock and hip-hop. 'We're just changing the lure. Kids today love rock music. We're giving them the music they like and understand.'[40] BGEA encourages young Christians to bring their friends for a day of entertainment, in the hope that they will 'accept Jesus'. 'Please pray that many youth would come to hear Franklin Graham present the gospel. You can make it possible for non-Christian youth to attend by donating $10 for one ticket, $50 for five, or $100 for 10. Imagine a young person's life changing forever, because you helped him or her attend Rock the River!'[41]

Festivals in Canada's Edmonton, Calgary and Fraser Valley venues, featured a number of rock bands. The line-up for Winnipeg, advertised as a 'high-octane youth-oriented evangelistic outreach', featured a number of rock bands, including *Thousand Foot Krutch, Starfield, Fresh IE, The Letter Black* and *Flame*. While this five-hour event was free, a $25 Rock Zone pass could be purchased that included an exclusive Rock Zone T-shirt and privileged access close to the stage.[42]

'Rock the UK' was another BGEA evangelistic programme based on rock music. It featured high-energy, large-scale music concerts aimed specifically at the under-25s. The first event was 'Rock Thurrock', advertised as 'three hours of Hip-Hop, Rock and R&B [rhythm and blues] from bands *LZ7*, *Empire Nation* and *Beautiful Remnant'*, plus a message of hope from Will Graham, Billy's grandson. BGEA issued this invitation: 'We would love for you to join us for this exciting event which will be full of high-energy and dynamic music with a powerful gospel message from Will Graham. Tickets £10.00 per person.'[43]

BGEA festivals have become a showpiece for the contemporary Christian music scene. They are overwhelmingly ecumenical, charismatic, shallow, and worldly; they are dominated by deafening rock music with its thundering beat that induces great excitement among the expectant audience. Most bands use powerful strobe lighting, popularised by the club scene during the 1960s, when it was used to enhance the effects of LSD trips. The effect is to maximise the crashing sounds of heavy metal, producing rhythmic waving of arms and ecstatic jumping among exuberant fans. Then the music stops, the rocking, dancing and flashing lights cease, and Franklin Graham or his son Will, present a message that is supposed to be relevant to the youth of today. The BGEA claims that thousands of young people have 'accepted Jesus' during these events. Sadly, many of the young people who 'accept Jesus' in the emotional atmosphere of a musical rave have not genuinely repented of their sin, are not truly born again and therefore are not saved. This is the tragedy of the BGEA's worldly festival evangelism.

These festivals surely represent the true legacy of Billy Graham's compromised ministry. The compromise that started gradually in the 1950s, has gathered pace over the years. We now see an organisation that is trivialising the faith once delivered to the saints—an organisation that has fallen in love with the ways and practices of the world. The BGEA that launched the Lausanne Movement for world evangelization four decades ago has degenerated into an organisation that promotes 'Christian' rock concerts, charges admission fees, and presents a watered-down version of the Gospel. We must understand that the Lausanne Movement has grown out of the vague doctrinal beliefs of its founder. Graham's rejection of Reformed Christian doctrine, his failure to separate from false teaching, his eager embrace of worldliness, his ready acceptance of the Church of Rome, and his endorsement of ecumenism have had a profound and lasting influence on the Lausanne Movement.

(Endnotes)

1 *Christianity Today*, 'Can Evangelicalism Survive Its Success?' Oct. 5, 1992, cited from *Billy Graham and Rome* by David Cloud, Way of Life Literature, second edition 2009, p4

2 *Bookstore Journal*, November 1991, cited from *Billy Graham and Rome* by David Cloud, Way of Life Literature, second edition 2009, p44

3 Graham's letter to the Executive Committee, Greater New York Evangelistic Campaign, 29 May, 1951, http://www2.wheaton.edu/bgc/archives/exhibits/NYC57/02sample08.htm

4 Ernest Pickering, *The Tragedy of Compromise*, Bob Jones University Press, 1994, p55

5 Carol George, *God's Salesman – Norman Vincent Peale and the Power of Positive Thinking*, Oxford University Press, 1993, p145

6 George M Marsden, *Reforming Fundamentalism*, William B Eerdmans Publishing, 1995 edition, p162

7 Iain H Murray, *Evangelism Divided*, The Banner of Truth, 2000, p29

8 Carol George, *God's Salesman*, 1993, p147

9 *Christianity Today*, 'Billy Does It Again, New York celebrates Graham's enduring importance.' By Tony Carnes in Queens, New York, posted 6/28/2005, 12:00AM

10 *Christianity Today*, 'One Last Gotham Visit for Billy Graham, The evangelist's upcoming New York crusade recalls his historic confrontation with segregation, fundamentalism, and mainline theology nearly 50 years ago.' Collin Hansen, posted 8/08/2008 12:33PM

11 'Should Fundamentalists Support the Billy Graham Crusades' (1957), a pamphlet written by Dr. Ernest Pickering, published by the Independent Fundamental Churches of America, p8

12 Ibid. p10

13 Ibid. p17

14 *Christianity Today*, 1 April 1957, cited from the pamphlet 'Should Fundamentalists Support the Billy Graham Crusades', p7

15 The Episcopal Address was read by Bishop Gerald Kennedy, Sunday night, April 26, 1964. http://methodistthinker.com/2010/04/19/podcast-bishop-gerald-kennedy-on-the-marks-of-a-methodist/

16 The Middletown Bible Church, 'Problems of Ecumenical Evangelism, Is Billy Graham Right or Wrong?', article under Doctrinal studies, www.middletownbiblechurch.org/separate/billgram.htm

17 *The Assimilation of Evangelist Billy Graham Into the Roman Catholic Church* by Wilson Ewin, Quebec Baptist Missions, Quebec, Canada. A book review by Pastor EL Bynum, pastor of Tabernacle Baptist Church and editor of the Plains Baptist Challenger in Lubbock Texas, cited in *The Baptist Pillar*

18 Documented in David Cloud's book, *Evangelicals and Rome*, Way of Life Literature, 1999

19 *Saturday Evening Post*, Jan./Feb. 1980, Billy Graham, 'The Pilgrim Pope: A Builder of Bridges' cited from *Billy Graham and Rome*, Way of Life Literature, second edition 2009, p73

20 *U.S. News & World Report*, Dec 19, 1988, cited from His Sheep website, Politician? Preacher? Prophet? Or A Heretic? http://www.hissheep.org/catholic/billy_graham_politician_preacher_prophet_heretic.html

21 Proclamation, Invitation, & Warning website, Billy Graham, http://procinwarn.com/billy.htm

22 Billy Graham in *Christianity Today*, Editorial: 'Standing Firm, Moving Forward', 16 September 1996

23 From 'The Gospel That Saves' by Dave Hunt, January 1998, cited from website of Reaching Catholics For Christ, http://www.reachingcatholics.org/gospels.html

24 Sir David Frost, Billy Graham in Conversation, May 30, 1997, pp. 68, 143, cited from *Billy Graham and Rome*, Way of Life Literature, second edition 2009, p93

25 Billy Graham, *Just as I am*, Zondervan, 1977, p277

26 Ibid. p489

27 Ibid. p482

28 Ibid. p484

29 'A Call to Separation and Unity: D. Martyn Lloyd-Jones and "Evangelical Unity"' by Mark Sidwell, *Detroit Baptist Seminary Journal*, (Fall 1998): 35–62, p43

30 *Baptist Studies Bulletin*, August 2006, No. 5 Vol. 8, 'In Response To… Billy Graham on the Mystery of Salvation' by Bruce Gourley

31 Ibid. Quoted from the above article

32 The Templeton Prize website, http://www.templetonprize.org/purpose.html

33 Robert Schuller, *Self-Esteem, the New Reformation*, Word Books, 1982 p47

34 TV interview of Billy Graham by Robert Schuller, Hour Of Power, Part 1, an approximately 7 minute long Broadcast in Southern California on Saturday, May 31, 1997.

35 Sir David Frost, Billy Graham in Conversation, May 30, 1997, transcript of an interview with David Frost, cited from Seek God website, Deceptions: Graham, Peale & Schuller, http://www.seekgod.ca/deceptions.htm

36 William Martin, *A Prophet with Honor - The Billy Graham Story*, Harper Perennial, 1992, p.574.

37 Billy Graham, *Answers to Life's Problems*, Thomas Nelson, 1988, p278

38 Tony Snow Interviews Billy Graham, Show: Fox News Sunday, January 2, 2000, cited from http://www.deceptioninthechurch.com/graham2.html

39 David Cloud, *Billy Graham and Rome*, Way of Life Literature, second edition 2009, p114

40 *Quad City Times*, Aug. 9, 2009, cited from August 14, 2009, 'Franklin Graham: Minister of Christ or Priest of Baal?' by Ralph Ovadal, http://www.pccmonroe.org/neo-evangelicalism/2009.08.14.htm.

41 Canadian Christianity website, 'Rock the River bands set to shake things up' by Shara Lee, 24 September 2011, http://canadianchristianity.com/bc/bccn/0710/17bands.html

42 Billy Graham Evangelistic Association website. Festivals and Celebrations, http://www.billygraham.org/articlepage.asp?articleid=8089

43 Billy Graham Evangelistic Association UK website, Our Ministries, Rock Thurrock, Main event

Chapter 3

John Stott – the political theologian

While the Lausanne Movement was built on the reputation and charisma of Billy Graham, it was the political and organisational skills of John Stott that guided and directed the Movement. Stott acted as chairman of the drafting committee for the Lausanne Covenant, and was also chairman of the Lausanne Theology and Education Group from 1974 to 1981. These positions of influence allowed him to move Lausanne in a direction that embraced the belief that evangelism and social action are a partnership, to quote Stott's analogy, 'like two blades of a pair of scissors or two wings of a bird'.[1]

John Stott had studied theology at Ridley Hall Theological College, Cambridge, and in 1945 was ordained to the Anglican ministry. In the early 1950s he was appointed curate and then rector at All Souls Church, Langham Place, London, the church in which he spent most of his life. In 1954 Stott was actively involved in Billy Graham's Greater London Crusade and began a close personal friendship with Graham, a relationship that would continue through the rest of Stott's ministry and life.[2] He was appointed a Chaplain to Her Majesty Queen Elizabeth II in 1959.

John Stott's ecumenical vision was enlarged through his engagement with the World Council of Churches and with the Roman Catholic Church. In 1968 he attended the World Council conference at Uppsala, Sweden, as an observer and adviser, and was deeply moved by a speech on world poverty.[3] From the early 1970s Stott became increasingly involved in projects outside All Souls. Consequently, in 1975 he resigned as rector and was appointed Rector Emeritus. In 1974 he had founded The Langham Partnership International, which was known as John Stott Ministries in the USA. In 1982, he also founded the London Institute for Contemporary Christianity. Such was Stott's status among evangelical Christians worldwide that in 2005 *Time* magazine ranked him among the 100 most influential people in the world.[4] He was honoured with the CBE in The Queen's 2006 New Year Awards.

Billy Graham called John Stott the most respected clergyman in the world. Graham wrote: 'I can't think of anyone who has been more effective in introducing so many people to a biblical worldview. He represents a touchstone of authentic biblical scholarship that, in my opinion, has scarcely been paralleled since the days of the 16th century European Reformers.'[5] The Christian biographer John Pollock described him as 'the theological leader of world evangelicalism'. His books, especially *The Cross of Christ* (1986) and *Basic Christianity* (1996), have been standard works and best-sellers among evangelical Christians. Although John Stott has been widely recognised as a great Christian leader, theologian, and writer on Christian apologetics, as well as a very gifted preacher, few Christians know anything about Stott's political ideology. We do need to look beyond Stott's theological writings, for as we shall see, the outworking of his political convictions has played a significant role in shaping the Lausanne Movement.

The evangelical divide

A defining moment of Stott's career came in October 1966 when he was chairing a meeting of the National Assembly of Evangelicals. Doctor Martyn Lloyd-Jones, widely regarded as the leading evangelical preacher of his day, had been invited to give the keynote address at the opening session of the Assembly. In his address, later entitled 'Evangelical Unity: An Appeal', Lloyd-Jones contended that evangelicals had not done enough to protest the unscriptural tendencies in the ecumenical movement. As a strong believer in evangelical unity, he said the answer was for evangelicals to leave the compromised denominations and form their own grouping. Faithful ministers of the present day, he said, 'are the representatives and the successors of the glorious men who fought this same fight, the good fight of faith in centuries past. We are standing in the position of the Protestant Reformers.'[6]

When Lloyd-Jones finished speaking John Stott took the podium, and in an impromptu speech, to the surprise of all present, virtually rebuked the Doctor. His actual words were: 'I believe history is against what Dr Lloyd-Jones has said… Scripture is against him… I hope no one will act precipitately…'[7] According to Rev Robert Horn, 'The atmosphere was electric, none of us had seen an occasion like it—the two leading Evangelicals of the day differing in public over a matter of such practical importance.'[8]

Alan Gibson, long-time Secretary of the British Evangelical Council, recalled that the Lloyd-Jones' appeal was rejected, not because of his passionate manner, but because John Stott and others disagreed with the content of what he had said. Basil Howlett, who witnessed the event, wrote in the British Evangelical Council newsletter, 'The ecumenical movement was on the march and anyone who stood apart was regarded as a fool or a fanatic. Against that backcloth, Lloyd-Jones made his impassioned plea for evangelicals, divided among the denominations, to come together "as a fellowship or association of evangelical churches", and to stand together for the gospel. The words "separate" and "secede" were not mentioned. It was a positive appeal for evangelicals to stand together, not just occasionally but always.' His burden was that the ecumenical movement was endangering the Gospel itself, and an opportunity existed for churches sharing that very concern to act together.[9]

This watershed event marked the beginning of a deep rift between Anglican and non-Anglican evangelicals, a rift which, in many ways, has not been overcome even to this day. Over the remaining years of Lloyd-Jones' life the theological divide between Stott and him would grow into a chasm. Shortly before Lloyd-Jones' death in 1981, Stott requested a meeting with him that, according to Stott's own account, was an attempt at reconciliation with his former mentor. But the Doctor, who knew that both history and Scripture supported his position, while personally polite, made it clear that the divide between them was not one of personalities but of principles.[10]

What Lloyd-Jones did not appreciate was how deeply the ecumenical vision had penetrated the soul of John Stott and other evangelical Anglicans. Within six short months John Stott would become the Chairman and the driving force of the First National Evangelical Anglican Congress (NEAC1) which convened at Keele in Staffordshire in April 1967. The Archbishop of Canterbury, Dr Michael Ramsay, a liberal Anglo-Catholic, was invited to give the opening address. To the obvious delight of the

Archbishop, who had officially visited the Pope in the Vatican in 1966, the Congress expressed a positive attitude to ecumenism—'We desire to enter this ecumenical dialogue fully. We are no longer content to stand apart from those with whom we disagree.'[11] The Congress ended by affirming the apparent ground rule for all ecumenical dialogue, namely, that anyone who confesses Christ as God and Saviour must be accepted as a Christian—all engaged in ecumenism 'have a right to be treated as Christians'.[12] This new enthusiasm for ecumenism on the part of evangelical Anglicans was the main outcome of the Congress. John Stott warned the Congress: 'Evangelicals in the Church of England are changing too... We have acquired a reputation for narrow partisanship and obstructionism... We need to repent and change.'[13]

In obedience to Stott's appeal, evangelical Anglicans appeared to have changed their view of the Reformation by the time of the second NEAC2 (1977) in Nottingham. Again under the leadership of John Stott, the Congress confidently asserted that 'the Church on earth is marked out by Baptism, which is complete sacramental initiation into Christ and his body.'[14] In response to the second Vatican Council (1962-65) the Congress affirmed: 'Seeing ourselves and Roman Catholics as fellow-Christians, we repent of attitudes that have seemed to deny it.'[15] In a statement of monumental significance, Stott was going so far as to define the Church as the community of those baptized, a view of the Church that is wholly consistent with the post-Vatican II teachings of Rome. It was now clear that Stott's view of the Church and Lloyd-Jones' view (a body of believers justified by faith in Christ alone) were fundamentally different, and this was the actual reason for the division in October 1966. To put it another way, Lloyd-Jones still believed in the doctrines of the Reformation, while Stott did not— and this was the real cause of the division.

In order to understand the thinking and politics of John Stott, we must recognise that at heart he was an ecumenist who was keen to work alongside the Church of Rome. He was also deeply committed to the compromised doctrines of new evangelicalism. Indeed, we may even regard him as the prototype 'new evangelical' described in chapter 1 (see page 3). In this chapter we look at his low view of Scripture, which allowed him to follow a theistic view of evolution, and we shall hear his reasons for dissociating himself from fundamentalism. We shall also spend some time examining his political agenda and his passion for reunion with Rome.

Stott's low view of Scripture

John Stott was perfectly comfortable working alongside the theologians of Fuller Theological Seminary, despite their compromised view on the inerrancy of Scripture. In chapter 1 we saw that Daniel Fuller, Dean of the Seminary, promoted the idea that there are two kinds of Scripture—revelational Scripture that is wholly without error and non-revelational Scripture that is not.[16] By the end of the 1960s, 'limited inerrancy' was the dominant view of the Seminary. Yet Stott was perfectly willing to work with theologians from Fuller Seminary in driving forward the agenda of the Lausanne Movement.

Stott's method of interpreting Scripture allowed him to accept the theory of evolution as consistent with biblical revelation. Throughout most of his life as a theologian he believed and taught an evolutionary version of creation from the first chapters of Genesis. In an article in *The Church of England Newspaper* in 1968, he wrote: 'It seems perfectly possible to reconcile the historicity of Adam with at least some (theistic) evolutionary theory. Many biblical Christians in fact do so, believing them to be not entirely incompatible. To assert the historicity of an original pair who sinned through disobedience is one thing; it is quite another to deny all evolution and assert the separate and special creation of everything, including both subhuman creatures and Adam's body. The suggestion (for it is no more than this) does not seem to me to be against Scripture and therefore impossible that when God made man in His own image, what He did was to stamp His own likeness on one of the many "hominoids" which appear to have been living at the time.'[17]

In 1986 Paul Taylor, a high school science teacher with a masters degree in chemistry, heard Stott's presentation on his recently published book *The Cross of Christ* (1986). In public, Taylor asked Stott how he reconciled his belief in theistic evolution with his strongly stated conviction that Adam was a real historical figure. According to Taylor, Stott 'answered with his now-famous *homo divinus* analogy, claiming that the "dust of the earth" from which Adam was made, was the evolutionary process, guided by God, whereby man evolved from ape-like ancestors. It was his contention that Adam was basically the first evolved ape — or rather first evolved from the ape-like common ancestor. Into this ape-like Adam, God breathed his soul.'[18]

In *Understanding the Bible: Expanded Edition* (1999), Stott attempts to justify his evolutionary views. 'But my acceptance of Adam and Eve as historical is not incompatible with my belief that several forms of pre-Adamic "hominid" may have existed for thousands of years previously. These hominids began to advance culturally. They made their cave drawings and buried their dead. It is conceivable that God created Adam out of one of them. You may call them *Homo erectus*. I think you may even call some of them *Homo sapiens*, for these are arbitrary scientific names. But Adam was the first *Homo divinus*, if I may coin a phrase, the first man to whom may be given the biblical designation "made in the image of God".'[19]

So in direct contradiction of Scripture, Stott says that as 'hominids began to advance culturally... [it] is conceivable that God created Adam out of one of them'. Scripture says, 'And the Lord God formed man of the dust of the ground' (Genesis 2.7). This tells us a lot about Stott's view of Scripture, for he is prepared to disregard the clear teaching of Scripture when it does not support his worldview. His teaching on evolution has had a powerful effect on the thinking of many Christians, especially young people, who now accept theistic evolution as an article of faith. Undoubtedly Stott's theistic evolution made him intellectually respectable in the eyes of the world.

In *Evangelical Essentials* (1988), Stott appeared to waver over the question of the doctrine of eternal punishment in hell. 'Emotionally, I find the concept intolerable and do not understand how people can live with it without either cauterising their feelings or cracking under the strain. But our emotions are a fluctuating, unreliable guide to truth and must not be exalted to the place of supreme authority in determining it . . . my question must be – and is – not what does my heart tell me, but what does God's word say?'[20] But later in his career Stott appeared to have clarified his thinking and seemed to place his emotions above Scripture by developing a doctrine of annihilationism that denied the Bible's clear statements on eternal punishment.[21]

Stott was always sympathetic to the cause of woman's ordination in the Church of England. He believed that it is 'biblically permissible for women to teach men, provided that the content of their teaching is biblical, its context a team and its style humble'.[22] His position is based on the idea that God gives gifts to both men and women, and therefore women should be encouraged to use their gifts. He writes: 'If God endows women with spiritual gifts (which he does), and thereby calls them to exercise their gifts for the common good (which he does), then the church must recognize God's gifts and calling, must make appropriate spheres of service available to women, and should "ordain" (that is, commission and authorize) them to exercise their God-given ministry, at least in team situations.'[23] There is no doubt that Stott's endorsement of ordination for women as deacons and 'presbyters' (essentially local ministers), as long as they were not in positions of 'headship', swayed many within the Church of England to accept this development. In fact it was evangelicals who swayed the vote in 1992, and that is why there are now nearly 3,000 women clergy in the Church of England. John Stott's illogical corresponding position that they should not be in pastoral oversight has of course predictably been ignored.[24]

Stott's repudiation of fundamentalism

Stott was deeply antagonistic towards traditional evangelicals, whom he disparagingly labelled 'fundamentalists', reserving the term 'evangelical' for himself and other like-minded 'new evangelicals'. In *Essentials: A liberal-Evangelical Dialogue* (1988), he provides a list of 'eight tendencies of the mind-set styled fundamentalism' from which he wishes to dissociate himself.

First on Stott's list is the assertion that fundamentalists have 'a general suspicion of scholarship and science, which sometimes degenerates into a thoroughgoing anti-intellectualism'. Dr Peter Masters, pastor of the Metropolitan Tabernacle, London, recognising Stott as a committed theistic evolutionist, responds: 'The absurdity of this could be demonstrated at length, but what is probably meant is that fundamentalists accept God's act of creation in six days as opposed to the theory of evolution.'[25]

Stott dissociates himself from 'a mechanical view or "dictation theory" of biblical inspiration, with a consequent denial of the human, cultural element in Scripture and therefore of the need for "biblical criticism" and careful hermeneutics'. Masters responds that 'fundamentalists believe in the total inspiration and authority of the Bible, the message of which was in no way distorted by the ignorance or culture of its human authors. New evangelicals, however, have a very low view of scriptural authority, having absorbed many of the humanistic views of liberals about the formation of the Bible.'[26]

Another problem for Stott is that fundamentalists adopt 'a literalistic interpretation of all Scripture… leading to an insufficient recognition of the place of poetry, metaphor and symbol'. Masters says this is a deeply serious issue. 'Over the years new evangelicals (intimidated by liberalism) have plunged into an increasingly "secular" approach to Bible interpretation in which an obsessively technical analysis of the text has ousted the Bible's own rules of interpretation (so well articulated at the time of the Reformation).'[27]

Stott declares that fundamentalists adopt 'a separatist ecclesiology, together with a blanket repudiation of the Ecumenical Movement and the World Council of Churches'. As a committed ecumenist, he dissociates himself from reformed Christians who reject the ecumenical movement and the liberalism of the World Council of Churches. Here we should remember the Nottingham Conference of 1977, chaired by Stott, which asserted: 'Seeing ourselves and Roman Catholics as fellow-Christians, we repent of attitudes that have seemed to deny it.'[28] It seems more than strange that Stott, who accepts Roman Catholics as fellow Christians, is not able to accept reformed Bible-believing Christians, who actually believe the fundamentals of the faith and promote the doctrines of the Reformation, as fellow Christians.

Stott goes even further, accusing fundamentalists of 'some extreme right-wing political concerns'.[29] Here we have a dyed-in-the-wool socialist, who openly supports a radical left-wing political agenda, as we shall see below, accuse his reformed theological opponents of right-wing politics. Surely there is more than an element of hypocrisy in this accusation. But not in Stott's mind, for those who do not support his socialist agenda are branded as having extreme right-wing concerns.

Masters responds by saying that fundamentalists, in obedience to the great commission, make the work of soul-winning their highest priority, 'believing that this is the greatest work of compassion, and all other acts of compassion will flow from converted hearts. New evangelicals, however, underestimate the power of the Holy Spirit to apply the Gospel to hearts, and believe they must secure a hearing by social activity.'[30]

Stott's political agenda

During a session at the Lausanne Cape Town 2010 Congress, Samuel Escobar and Rene Padilla, two pillars of the Latin American Theological Fraternity, recounted significant events and publications that had contributed to the Lausanne Movement. Samuel Escobar referred to the Lausanne Covenant of 1974, which he helped to draft with John Stott, and read from paragraph 9: 'All of us are shocked by the poverty of millions and disturbed by the injustices which cause it'. He said that at the time this statement was seen as so controversial that many people wanted to remove all references to the injustice which cause poverty. Influenced by the Latin American theologians, John Stott wrote in his exposition of the Covenant: 'It is our duty to be involved in socio-political action; that is, both in social action (caring for society's casualties) and in political action (concerned for the structures of society itself).'[31]

Rene Padilla told how John Stott had travelled all over Latin America to discuss issues of social concern that would later appear in the Lausanne Covenant. According to Escobar, John Stott said that his trip to Latin America helped to change some of his views and the way he read the Scriptures. Rene Padilla expressed his concern about what he called an unjust economic system that he said is 'destroying humankind, affecting people all over the world but especially the poor'.[32]

Ronald Sider's influence on Stott

Another theologian who had a highly significant impact on the thinking and political views of John Stott was Professor Ronald Sider, the founder of Evangelicals for Social Action, a think tank which aims to develop solutions to social and economic problems. Sider's political views are expressed in *Rich Christians in an Age of Hunger* (1977), which *Christianity Today* described as one of the most important books of the 20th century. According to Wikipedia, Ronald Sider 'is often identified by others with the Christian left, though he personally disclaims any political inclination'.[33]

Sider's views expressed in *Rich Christians* struck a chord with Stott, and this allowed the two men to work closely together on the Lausanne paper on simple lifestyles, as we shall see below. The basic premise of *Rich Christians* is that Third World poverty is caused by the selfishness and exploitation of Christians in the rich West. Sider asserts that Christians in the affluent West have become entangled in a complex web of institutional sin. 'If God's Word is true then all of us who dwell in affluent nations are trapped in sin. We have profited from systematic injustice... We are guilty of an outrageous offense against God and neighbor.'[34] In Sider's simplistic view all Christians in the West are trapped in sin, for the economic system that has made them affluent (capitalism) is a system that produces systematic injustice. He calls on Christians in the West to repent. 'The One who stands ready to forgive us for our sinful involvement in terrible economic injustice offers us his grace to begin living a radically new lifestyle of identification with the poor and oppressed.'[35]

Sider also calls for the redistribution of wealth to help the poor and oppressed in the developing world. He suggests that Christians should celebrate a modern Jubilee. In 1980 he said that if 'all Christians worldwide would pool all their stocks, bonds, and income producing property and businesses and redistribute them equally... the world would be startled.' The evangelistic impact of such an act would be fantastic and 'might indeed convince millions that Jesus was from the Father'.[36]

Sider claims that 'biblical revelation tells us that God and his faithful people are always at work liberating the oppressed and also provide some principles apropos of justice in society'.[37] He interprets the biblical narrative of the Exodus as an example of the oppressed people of the world being liberated through political action. He says that God 'acted to free a poor oppressed people... the liberation of a poor, oppressed people was right at the heart of God's design.'[38] Sider concludes, 'The God of the Bible wants to be known as the liberator of the oppressed... the Lord of the universe was at work correcting oppression and liberating the poor.'[39]

But Sider's interpretation of Exodus is way off the mark, for he is simply using Scripture to support his political views. The real emphasis of Exodus is the theology of the history of the salvation of his chosen people—the people of God are saved by the blood of the Passover lamb. The apostle Paul viewed the death of the Passover lamb as fulfilled in Christ—the Lamb of God who shed his blood to save his people from the guilt and power of sin. 'For even Christ our Passover is sacrificed for us' (1 Corinthians 5.7). But Sider sees the message of Exodus as political and not spiritual.

Sider uses Scripture to cultivate the idea that God is on the side of the poor. He says that cross-cultural missionaries 'must carefully and fully expound for new converts the explosive biblical message that God is on the side of the poor and oppressed.'[40] In his chapter on 'God and the Poor', Sider raises the impertinent question in bold capitals: 'IS GOD A MARXIST?'[41] He then discusses, in some detail, how 'the God of the Bible wreaks horrendous havoc on the rich', but he does not answer his own question. So the reader is left with the outrageous suggestion that perhaps God is a Marxist, or at least sympathetic to Marxist ideology.

Yet Scripture is clear that God is no respecter of persons (Romans 2.11). The great God, who is God of gods and Lord of lords, shows no partiality and takes no bribes (Deuteronomy 10.17). Therefore, the people of God 'shall not be partial to the poor, nor honour the person of the mighty' (Leviticus 19.15). The Wisdom literature says that 'it is not good to show partiality in judgment' (Proverbs 24.23). The reputation of the Lord Jesus was that he did not show favouritism, but taught the way of God in truth (Luke 20.21). The apostle Peter, a Jew, was sent by God to preach the Gospel at the house of Cornelius, a Gentile. Peter opened his message with these words, 'In truth, I perceive that God shows no partiality' (Acts 10:34). The Lord Jesus supped with both the poor and the rich; he showed compassion to both the poor blind beggar and the rich tax collector Zacchaeus.

Sider declares that 'the explosive message of the prophets is that God destroyed Israel because of mistreatment of the poor! The Word of the Lord is this: Economic exploitation sent the chosen people into captivity'[42] But Sider is misusing Scripture, for it is clear from Scripture that the great sin of Israel was idolatry. The kingdom of Israel was carried away captive into Assyria because of their idolatry: 'They followed idols, became idolaters, and went after the nations who were all around them... Therefore the Lord was very angry with Israel and removed them from his sight' (2 Kings 17.15, 18). Jeremiah records the idolatry of Judah that led to the Babylonian captivity (Jeremiah 32:29-35).

In *Productive Christians in an Age of Guilt Manipulators* (1981), David Chilton provides a biblical response to *Rich Christians*. He demonstrates that Sider's proposals for solving the problems of poverty are unbiblical to the core. 'He has substituted his own outline of social justice – an outline which more closely resembles Marx's Communist Manifesto than it does the book of Deuteronomy. He has called for dozens of interventionist and socialist programs which Scripture specifically forbids; he seems to assume that envy is a virtue; he writes of social problems, not in terms of sin, but of class war and hatred...'[43]

An article in *The Trinity Review* by Dr John W. Robbins, a reformed Presbyterian theologian and founder of The Trinity Foundation, says that Sider 'prefers to believe and teach the Marxist mythology that other countries are poor largely because America has exploited them and become rich. It is not widespread hunger that distinguishes this age; it is unprecedented prosperity. Sider is hostile to that prosperity and to the political-economic system that produced it—capitalism. He dreams of prosperity without the rich, food for all without the food producers. God promises to prosper those who obey him, and the prosperity of the West is obvious evidence of God's faithfulness. Sider regards it as evidence of our immorality.'[44]

Robbins concludes: 'Sider's message is not the message of the Bible; neither his economics nor his ethics can be called Christian. He has misled many through his selective citing of statistics and Scripture... Like many advocates of the socialist gospel before him, he twists the Scriptures to his own destruction. Unfortunately, that destruction is not merely his own, but all those who follow him. We may hope that his influence ends swiftly and permanently.'[45]

It is abundantly clear that Sider is promoting a radical socialist political agenda, dressed up in 'Christian' garb. His thesis that poverty in the so-called Third World is caused by rich Christians in the West is so ridiculous as to be laughable. Sider entirely ignores the blessings that come from a biblical work ethic and obedience to God's Word. The biblical view of poverty is considered in chapter 9.

Stott and Sider work together on the simple lifestyle

Sider's ability to use Scripture in a way that provided support for his socialist views had a great appeal for Stott. And so it was no surprise that in 1980 a working group was set up under the Lausanne banner, co-ordinated by Ronald Sider and under the chairmanship of John Stott, 'to study simple living in relation to evangelism, relief and justice, since all three are mentioned in the Lausanne Covenant's sentences on simple life-style.'[46]

Under the influence of Sider and Stott, participants in the working group were moved to repentance for their complicity in world injustice. They felt deeply that world evangelism was stifled and compromised by their complacency about social injustice. As Christians they were conscious of their 'own involvement in creating, perpetuating and allowing misery, poverty, destruction and irresponsibility to continue in the world... we can no longer separate ourselves because of distance from the poverty of the world, we must take the only other course – we must repent.'[47] How can Christians from the West evangelize people in developing nations if they perceive their own multi-national corporations to be exploiting them?

The justice theme was a big issue for participants. Ronald Sider said that relief and development were not enough. 'One of the most urgent agenda items for the church in the industrialised nations is to help our people begin honestly to explore to what extent our abundance depends on international economic structures that are unjust... Unless we grapple with that systemic question, our discussion of simple lifestyle has not gone beyond Christmas baskets and superficial charity which at times can even be, consciously or unconsciously, a philanthropic smoke screen diverting the oppressed from the structural causes of their poverty and our affluence.'

Shocked by the poverty of millions and disturbed by the injustice which they believed causes it, the working group agreed that the Church must stand with God and the poor against injustice. 'One quarter of the world's population enjoys unparalleled prosperity, while another quarter endures grinding poverty. This gross disparity is an intolerable injustice—we refuse to acquiesce in it. The call for a New International Economic Order expresses the justified frustration of the Third World.' It was agreed that 'personal and philanthropic endeavours are not enough; *political action is essential* to achieve fundamental structural change' (my italics). John Stott said: 'We become personally culpable when we acquiesce in the status quo by doing nothing.'[48] Thus the working group pointed Christians in two directions – personal commitment and political action – and urged a balance between the two.

An Evangelical Commitment to Simple Lifestyle, drafted by Stott and greatly influenced by Sider, was simply a regurgitation of the socialist message of *Rich Christians*. Christians in the West are held to be responsible for world poverty and therefore guilty of institutional sin. Their Christian duty is not only to redistribute resources to those living in poverty, but also to fight for a New International Economic Order.

Issues facing Christians

In his influential book, *Issues Facing Christians Today* (1990), Stott deals with the issue of what he calls North-South inequality. He says that although the United Nations endorsed the call by Third World countries for a New International Economic Order in 1974, little progress has been made to implement these proposals. He argues that North-South inequality is not God's fault, for he has provided resources in earth and sea.[49] Stott says that 'we need to pray that God will call more of his people to develop new international economic policies, work for political solutions, and give their lives in the field of Third World development, practical philanthropy and evangelism... We should ensure that our daily [news] paper has adequate Third World coverage, and perhaps subscribe to a magazine devoted to Third World needs and join the World Development Movement.'[50]

Another issue Stott considers is the role of the Church with regard to work and unemployment. He says that many Christians need to change their attitude 'towards the unemployed, and persuade the public to do the same. Those who have been schooled in the values of the so-called Protestant work ethic (industry, honesty, resourcefulness, thrift, etc) tend to despise those who are losers in the struggle to survive, as if it were their fault.' Stott, having little time for the Protestant work ethic, says the

Church can help the unemployed by opening a drop-in centre on church premises, by sponsoring a scheme suggested by the Manpower Services Commission and by creating a new job at the church in administration or maintenance.[51]

In an essay in *Christianity Today*, entitled 'Creative by Creation: Our Need for Work', Stott says that although successive governments in Britain have done much to create jobs by methods of tax induce-ment, regional policies, retraining, and subsidies, 'in areas of serious unemployment, Christians ought not to hesitate to lobby parliament-arians, local authorities, industrialists, employers, union officials, and others to create more employment opportunities.'[52] John W Robbins, commenting on the essay, hit the mark by referring to Stott as a British socialist.[53]

Stott explains that he only truly understood the damage caused by racism when he read *The Autobiography of Malcolm X*. Stott writes that the red-hot anger of Malcolm X 'was due in part to "the world's most monstrous crime" of slavery, in part to the black American's eco-nomic dependence on white America, but above all to the humiliation caused by the white man's "malignant superiority complex".'[54] Here we should note that Malcolm X, whose writing has had such a large impact on Stott's thinking, was a minister of the Nation of Islam, a movement that teaches black pride and the principles of Islam. As a human rights activist Malcolm X advocated the complete separation of African Americans from white people, for he asserted that history proves that the white man is a devil. Yet Stott's study guide in *Issues*, 'The Multi-Racial Dream', recommends *The Autobiography of Malcolm X* as helpful reading for those who want to study the subject in more depth.[55, 56] It is disturbing that Stott's political views have been influ-enced by a radical like Malcolm X.

In his exposition of the Lausanne Covenant, Stott called upon political leaders to guarantee the freedoms that 'have been set forth in the Universal Declaration of Human Rights, which was unanimously adopted by the General Assembly of the United Nations in December 1948.'[57] His hope 'is that in the future, evangelical leaders will ensure that their social agenda includes such vital but controversial topics as halting climate change, eradicating poverty, abolishing armouries of mass destruction, responding adequately to the AIDS pandemic, and asserting the human rights of women and children in all cultures.'[58]

In *The Incomparable Christ* (2001), Stott writes that '[We] may well feel ashamed that we were not in the vanguard of the liberation movement, and that we did not develop an evangelical liberation theology.'[59] There is little doubt that Stott's political ideas are entirely consistent with a socialist ideology. He openly worked with liberation theologians and the socialist agenda of Ronald Sider. He actively sought a new economic order, he believed passionately in the redistribution of wealth, he fully supported the UN's charter on human rights, he was committed to the green agenda, he was committed to the multi-racial dream and he believed that it is the role of the state to provide jobs. These are the ideas that have helped to shape the Lausanne Movement.

Rick Warren's devotion to Stott

Towards the end of his long career Stott formed a close relationship with Rick Warren, famous pastor of Saddleback Church, California, and author of *The Purpose Driven Life* (2002). In the summer of 2005, John Stott and Billy Graham joined in Rick Warren's open letter to President Bush, calling on him to support rock star Bono's 'Make Poverty History' campaign.[60] The purpose of this campaign was to persuade President Bush and other world leaders at the G8 summit in Edinburgh, Scotland, to help the world's poorest people and give a clear timetable for cancelling the debts owed by the poorest countries.

In October 2005 John Stott eagerly endorsed Warren's PEACE Plan when he was invited to preach at Saddleback Church. Stott stepped into the pulpit wearing 'a blue Hawaiian shirt, in the vein of Pastor Rick Warren. Stott said he liked his Saddleback shirt, but, unlike Rick, was wearing socks'.[61] The hope was that Warren's PEACE Plan (promote reconciliation, equip servant leaders, assist the poor, care for the sick, educate the next generation) would be the beginning of a New Reformation.

Such was the affinity between the two men that Warren wrote a foreword for the fiftieth anniversary edition of Stott's best-seller *Basic Christianity* (2008). In 2010 Rick Warren gave his wholehearted endorsement to the third Lausanne Congress, making it clear that he was a great supporter of Stott's version of Christianity that included a strong commitment to socio-political action. Undoubtedly, the two men shared a common view of the Christian faith. Warren explained his devotion to Stott: 'I believe he is among the three most influential Christians in the last half of the 20th Century, right alongside Billy Graham and Mother Teresa. There is no doubt that "Uncle John" has had a tremendous influence on my own life and ministry. He was one of my closest mentors and recently I flew to the UK just to pray for him and sit by his bed.'[62]

Stott's Common Word

An event that tells us much about Stott's real agenda occurred in October 2007, when a large number of prominent Muslim clerics, scholars and intellectuals signed a letter calling for peace between Muslims and Christians. Entitled 'A Common Word between Us and You', the Muslim letter urged followers of the two faiths to find common ground between Christianity and Islam.[63] A Christian letter of response, entitled 'Loving God and Neighbor Together', drafted by scholars at Yale Divinity School's Center for Faith and Culture and signed by John Stott and about 300 other Christian leaders, was featured in the *New York Times* in November 2007.[64]

The letter extended 'our own Christian hand in return, so that together with all other human beings we may live in peace and justice as we seek to love God and our neighbors'. The letter went on to affirm that what is common between Christians and Muslims lies 'in something absolutely central to both: love of God and love of neighbor... We applaud that "A Common Word between Us and You" stresses so insistently the unique devotion to one God, indeed the love of God, as the primary duty of every believer. God alone rightly commands our ultimate allegiance... We find it equally heartening that the God whom we should love above all things is described as being Love. In the Muslim tradition, God, "the Lord of the worlds," is "The Infinitely Good and All-Merciful." And the New Testament states clearly that "God is love" (1 John 4:8)... Since Muslims seek to love their Christian neighbors, they are not against them, the document encouragingly states. Instead, Muslims are with them. As Christians we resonate deeply with this sentiment.'

The letter concluded: 'The future of the world depends on our ability as Christians and Muslims to live together in peace. If we fail to make every effort to make peace and come together in harmony you correctly remind us that "our eternal souls" are at stake as well... It is with humility and hope that we receive your generous letter, and we commit ourselves to labor together in heart, soul, mind and strength for the objectives you so appropriately propose.'[65]

The Christian response was a deeply heretical document, for it suggested that Islam and Christianity are equivalent religions that worship the same God. It said nothing about the exclusiveness of the Christian faith—it did not declare to the Muslim world that it needed the Gospel of Christ; that there is no other salvation but in Christ alone, for there is no other name under heaven, given among men, whereby we must be saved (Acts 4.12).

Signatures to the Christian letter included Rev John Stott, Rector Emeritus, All Souls Church, London; Rev Christopher Wright, International Director, Langham Partnership, London; and Rick Warren, Senior Pastor Saddleback Church, CA.[66] The fact that Stott signed this letter tells us much about his theology of God—he actually affirmed that Christians and Muslims worship the same God. His assertion that the Lausanne Movement is for the evangelization of the world has a hollow ring, for he has signed a document that seeks peace with Islam, yet says nothing about preaching the Gospel of Christ to the Muslim world.

Stott's ecumenical agenda

As with Billy Graham, ecumenism has always been at the heart of John Stott's ministry. He has been an adviser to the World Council of Churches and at the forefront of the Evangelical-Catholic movement in Great Britain. In 1977 he told the second National Evangelical Anglican Congress in Nottingham that 'The visible unity of all professing Christians should be our goal... and evangelicals should join others in the Church of England in working towards full communion with the Roman Catholic Church.'[67] When Pope John Paul II visited England in 1982 and was invited to participate in an ecumenical service in Canterbury Cathedral, John Stott said, 'It seemed entirely right that the united service should include a recitation of the Apostles' Creed, and so a reaffirmation of our common baptismal faith.'[68]

Conclusion

From the above discussion it is clear that Stott exhibited all the attributes of a compromised new evangelical. His low view of Scripture allowed him to accept and promote a theistic view of evolution that has misled many evangelical Anglicans. Dispite his undoubted intellectual grasp of theology, he was so indifferent to sound doctrine that he was able to work along side the compromised agenda of Fuller Seminary. His socialist convictions allowed him to work with Ronald Sider's left-wing agenda, to promote the cause of climate change, and to call for a new international economic order. His ecumenical aspirations enabled him to overlook the false doctrines of Rome as he worked to undo the Reformation. Indeed, such was his love for Rome, and so much did he disown the Reformation, that he deliberately separated himself from reformed Christians, whom he unfairly labelled as fundamentalists with extreme right-wing concerns and unloving attitudes.

Guided by the ecumenical theology of Graham and Stott, the underlying philosophy of the Lausanne Movement is to include all who call themselves Christian, irrespective of what they actually believe. In chapter 1 we saw that the Lausanne Movement has linked evangelization and ecumenism. The Roman Church adopts a similar position: 'From its beginnings, the ecumenical movement has been closely connected with evangelization. Unity, in fact, is the seal of the credibility of missionary activity and so the Second Vatican Council noted with regret that the scandal of division "damages the most sacred cause of preaching".'[69]

While the Lausanne Movement is committed to the ecumenical agenda of Billy Graham and John Stott, it has been strangely silent about whether this includes union with Rome. The reason for this silence is the fear of driving away those evangelical Christians who still have sympathy with the doctrines of the Reformation. The hope is that over time reformed Christians will gradually come to accept that Lausanne's message of 'unity in love' means union with Rome. In the next chapter we hear more about Lausanne's hope for reunion with the Roman Catholic Church.

(Endnotes)

1 John Stott, *The Contemporary Christian*, Intervarsity Press, 1992, pp339-40
2 Billy Graham Center, Archives, Papers of John Robert Walmsley Stott - Collection 590

3 Article in *Fulcrum* by Graham King, Bishop of Sherborne, 'John Stott (1921-2011), More than Anglican but not Less', http://www.fulcrum-anglican.org.uk/page.cfm?ID=645

4 *Time* magazine, 'The 2005 Time 100, John Stott' by Billy Graham, Time online, 18 April 2005

5 Ibid.

6 Iain Murray, *D. Martyn Lloyd-Jones, The Fight of Faith, 1939-1981*, Banner of Truth Trust, 1990, p524

7 'A Call to Separation and Unity: D. Martyn Lloyd-Jones and "Evangelical Unity"' by Mark Sidwell, *Detroit Baptist Seminary Journal*, (Fall 1998): 35–62, p53

8 Robert Horn's comments appear in *Martyn Lloyd-Jones: Chosen by God*, Crossway Books (July 1986) by Christopher Catherwood, p22, cited from Detroit Baptist Seminary Journal, 'A Call to Separation and Unity: D. Martyn Lloyd-Jones and "Evangelical Unity"' by Mark Sidwell, (Fall 1998): 35–62

9 *Evangelicals Now*, October 1996, 'Thirty years of hurt? Putting the record straight concerning Dr Martyn Lloyd-Jones's 1996 address to the Evangelical Alliance' by Alan Gibson

10 An article by Dr Paul M Elliott 'How was Martyn Lloyd-Jones' stand on the basis of church unity received?', cited from Teaching the Word Ministries, www.teachingtheword.org

11 Keele 1967, 'The National Evangelical Anglican Congress Statement', ed Philip Crowe, 1967, p37

12 Ibid. p37

13 Ibid. p8

14 The Nottingham Statement (1977), the Official Statement of the second National Evangelical Anglican Congress held in April 1977

15 Ibid.

16 Harold Lindsell, *The Battle for the Bible*, Zondervan Publishing House, 1976, p113

17 John Stott, *The Church of England Newspaper*, June 17, 1968, cited by N.M. de S. Cameron, Evolution and the Authority of the Bible, quoted in Vital Apologetics Issues

18 Creation Science Evangelism website, article by Paul Taylor, 'Stott, Exegesis and Evolution', http://www.drdino.com/john-stott-exegesis-and-evolution/

19 John Stott, *Understanding the Bible: Expanded Edition*, Zondervan, 1999, pp54-56

20 John Stott, *Evangelical Essentials*, Hodder & Stoughton, 1988, p315-316.

21 Teaching the Word website, 'When calls for unity on biblical foundations fall on deaf ears' by Dr. Paul M. Elliott

22 John Stott, *Issues Facing Christians Today*, Marshall Pickering, 1990, p279

23 Ibid. p280

24 Thinking Anglicans website, comment posted by Robert Ian Williams, 29 July 2011

25 Peter Masters, 'Are we Fundamentalists?', *Sword and Trowel*, 1995, reprinted 2003, p31

26 Ibid. p15

27 Ibid. p16

28 Ibid. p17

29 Ibid. p31

30 Ibid. pp20-21

31 Lausanne Occasional Paper No. 3, 'The Lausanne Covenant: An Exposition and Commentary by John Stott', 1975, paragraph C, Doctrine of Salvation

32 Cited from Cape Town 2010 website, Plenary 3: session on 'World Faiths - Lausanne and Latin America - Samuel Escobar and Rene Padilla'

33 Wikipedia website, http://en.wikipedia.org/wiki/Ron_Sider#Criticism

34 Ronald Sider, *Rich Christians in an Age of Hunger*, Hodder and Stoughton, 1977, p145

35 Ibid. p144

36 Ibid. p84

37 Ibid. p179

38 Ibid. p54

39 Ibid. p55

40 Ibid. p182

41 Ibid. p64

42 Ibid. p55

43 David Chilton, *Productive Christians in an Age of Guilt-Manipulators*, Institute for Christian Economics, 1981, p43

44 *The Trinity Review*, March-April 1981, 'Ronald Sider Contra Deum' by John W. Robbins, p3

45 Ibid. p6

46 Lausanne Occasional Paper 20, 'An Evangelical Commitment to Simple Life-style', Introduction, http://www.lausanne.org/en/documents/lops/77-lop-20.html

47 Ibid. Stewardship

48 Ibid. Justice and Politics

49 John Stott, *Issues Facing Christians Today*, Marshall Pickering, 1990, p146

50 Ibid. p146

51 Ibid. p177

52 'Creative By Creation: Our Need for Work' in *Christianity Today* Vol 23, June 8, 1979b

53 *The Trinity Review*, November-December 1996, 'Our Comrades at Calvin College', John W. Robbins

54 John Stott, *Issues Facing Christians Today*, p221

55 Ibid. p415

56 Ibid. p387

57 Lausanne Occasional Paper 3: 'The Lausanne Covenant: An Exposition and Commentary by John Stott', 1975, paragraph C, Persecution

58 *Christianity Today*, 'Evangelism Plus, John Stott reflects on where we've been and where we're going', interview by Tim Stafford | posted 10/13/2006

59 John Stott, *The Incomparable Christ*, IVP, 2001, p108

60 *The New York Times*, 'A Preacher Who Tries To Deflect His Acclaim By Michael Luo', March 8, 2006, http://query.nytimes.com/gst/fullpage

61 John Stott at Saddleback: Lessons from a Hawaiian Shirt, by Kevin L. Howard, http://www.neednotfret.com/content/view/61/36/

62 My Friend, John Stott, Significantly Shaped My Ministry by Rick Warren, http://pastors.com/my-friend-john-stott-significantly-shaped-my-ministry/

63 Website of 'A Common Word between Us and You', http://www.acommonword.com/

64 *New York Times*, full page advertisement, 'Loving God and Neighbor Together: A Christian Response to A Common Word Between Us and You', www.acommonword.com/lib/downloads/fullpageadbold18.pdfCached

65 'Loving God and Neighbor Together: A Christian Response to A Common Word Between Us and You', http://www.yale.edu/faith/acw/acw.htm

66 Ibid.

67 Michael de Semlyen, *All Roads Lead to Rome?* 1993, Dorchester House Publications, p30

68 Malcolm Watts, 'The Crumbling of Evangelicalism', *Sword & Trowel*, 1987

69 Congregation for the Doctrine of the Faith, Doctrinal Note on some aspects of Evangelization, paragraph 12, cites John Paul II, Encyclical Letter Redemptoris mission, 1991. The Sovereign Pontiff Benedict XVI, in the Audience granted to the undersigned Cardinal Prefect on 6 October 2007, approved the present Doctrinal Note, adopted in the Ordinary Session of this Congregation, and ordered its publication.

Chapter 4

The Cape Town Congress 2010

In preparation for the third Lausanne Congress on World Evangelization in Cape Town in 2010, Fuller Theological Seminary hosted a gathering of the Lausanne Global Conversation on its Pasadena campus in March 2010. Douglas Birdsall, Executive Chair of the Lausanne Committee, commented: 'The changes in the church and the world necessitate a gathering like this.' Pastor Jim Belcher, author of *Deep Church: A Third Way Beyond Emerging and Traditional* (2009), led the 'conversation', focusing on the topic 'Culture Making: The Role of Christians in the World Today'. The gathering addressed issues such as the possible compromise of the Gospel in the face of culture, and the importance of culture making an addition to evangelism. In conclusion Dr Richard Mouw, the President of Fuller, said: 'Lausanne was a wonderful surprise in 1974 for those of us who felt confused and abandoned by evangelicalism—and I hope to be surprised again.'[1]

Lausanne III in Cape Town (2010) was endorsed by a number of prominent evangelical Christians. Rick Warren, Senior Pastor of Saddleback Church in the USA, author of *The Purpose Driven Life* and a member of the Cape Town advisory council, invited 'every Christian leader, church, denomination and believer—anyone who cares about reaching the world for Christ—to join hands and band together backing the 2010 Lausanne Congress. It's truly that important.'[2] He believed that the Cape Town Congress would prove to be a historical hinge point in the history of the Church. As a self-proclaimed world church leader, he begged all Christians to put aside petty differences and be a part of this historic event.[3]

John Stott, chief architect of The Lausanne Covenant and Honorary Chairman of the Lausanne Movement, gave this word: 'I praise God for the Lausanne Movement and as chairman of the Africa Host Committee it will be my privilege to welcome the Cape Town 2010 delegates to the continent of Africa. The church in Africa and also around the world needs the fresh stimulation and motivation to evangelism which this Congress will bring. The Congress will also equip us all in tackling the new issues and demanding challenges facing Christianity both here and world-wide.'[4]

Some of the most influential evangelicals in the world, including Rev Nicky Gumbel, pioneer of the Alpha Course at Holy Trinity, Brompton, London, and the influential pastors and theologians Dr Tim Keller, Dr Os Guinness and Pastor John Piper attended the Congress. Theology professor Ronald Sider, author of *Rich Christians in an Age of Hunger* (1977), was among those representing Palmer Theological Seminary from the USA. Also attending were a host of African Anglican bishops, including Archbishop Henry Orombi of Uganda. Other prominent personalities included evangelist Becky Pippert of Salt Shaker Ministries; evangelist Michael Ramsden from England; Vaughan Roberts, President of the Proclamation Trust and Rector of St Ebbe's Church, Oxford; Paul Eshleman of Campus Crusade for Christ; Richard Stearns of World Vision; and Michael Cassidy of African Enterprises.

The list of speakers, organisations and attendees was consistent with the ecumenical nature of the Lausanne Movement. While acknowledging that some denominations define evangelism differently from how it is described in the Lausanne Covenant, the Congress leaders said that 'attempts should be made to find people or groups that may be able to bridge this gap, especially among Catholic or Orthodox Christians. Attention should also be given to participants from para-church organisations.'[5]

The USA Council of Reference for the Cape Town Congress covered a wide spectrum of theological beliefs. Membership included Mr Jim Daly, President of Focus on the Family; Dr Steve Douglass, President of Campus Crusade for Christ; Dr Gary Haugen, President of International Justice Mission, a human rights agency; Dr Dean Hirsch, President of World Vision International; Dr Tim Keller, Pastor of Redeemer Presbyterian Church, New York; Dr Richard Mouw, President of

Fuller Theological Seminary; Dr David Neff, Editor, *Christianity Today*; Dr John Piper, theologian and Pastor of Bethlehem Baptist Church in Minneapolis, Minnesota; Mrs Becky Pippert, President of Salt Shaker Ministries; Dr Wess Stafford, President of Compassion International; Dr Mike Treneer, President of The Navigators; Dr Rick Warren, Pastor of Saddleback Church in Lake Forest, California; and Dr George Wood, General Superintendent of the Assemblies of God, USA.

Worship ceremonies shaped by Fuller Seminary

The opening and closing ceremonies of Cape Town 2010 were musical extravaganzas, with a large orchestra, massive choirs, colourful dance scenes, flowing banners, waving flags, a backdrop of projected images, flashing lights, rhythmic drumming, and much, much more. The overwhelming impression was that of the gathered emerging church at worship. (The emerging church is defined in chapter 5.)

We need to recognise that behind Lausanne's elaborate worship ceremonies was Fuller Seminary. We need to understand the role of the Brehm Center, founded in 2001 and funded by Fuller Trustee members William and Delores Brehm. The Center's mission, working as part of Fuller Seminary, 'is to revitalize the church and culture through the arts…'[6] The Center is committed to the ideals of the emerging church, and aims to empower and equip 'a new generation of Christian artists and church leaders to effectively integrate worship, theology, and the arts in order to enrich the encounter with God and the world'.[7]

Fuller Seminary eagerly grasped the opportunity offered by Lausanne III to propagate its new emerging concept of worship among the evangelicals gathered in Cape Town. Dr Ed Willmington, director of the Brehm Center, visited South Africa in order to make the sounds of the Congress as authentically African as possible. During his visit, as he prepared to serve as the conductor for the historic gatherings, he met those who were to be involved in the Cape Town ceremonies. He comments: 'There were dancers, drummers, banner carriers, children singers, two adult choirs, band members, soloists, an orchestra… and the list goes on. What a feeling in my soul when in October 2010 I raised my arms to start the music, knowing that when my arms dropped, all of these people were going to go into a highly coordinated set of actions – all planned to welcome people to their country and send them into the world to honour God and share the good news of the Gospel!'[8]

What is deeply disturbing about these ceremonies is that they have made the worship style of the emerging church acceptable to so many Christians across the world.

Lausanne's ecumenical agenda

The Lausanne Movement publicly demonstrated its ecumenical credentials by inviting the general secretary of the World Council of Churches (WCC) to address the Cape Town Congress. In his speech on the opening day Rev Olav Fykse Tveit, a Norwegian Lutheran theologian, said Christians of different traditions needed to participate together in God's mission, for they are called to be one. He explained that Dr Birdsall's invitation to greet dear friends in the Lausanne Movement reminded him what it was all about. 'This historic invitation is a sign that God has called all of us to the ministry of reconciliation and to evangelism. I am honoured to be here with a delegation from the World Council of Churches and to greet you on behalf of this global fellowship of Orthodox, Protestant, Old Catholic, Anglican and Pentecostal member churches. Many of you belong to these churches... I can see how much we share a common vision of the holistic mission of God. I am very encouraged by how evangelicals, churches and individuals share our calling as the WCC to address the needs of the whole human being and the whole of creation. *The distance between Lausanne and Geneva is not very far*, and it should not be. Let us keep the road open, and the dialogue going, so that we learn from one another how we can participate in God's mission together with respect to others as one Body of Christ. In this common journey it is important to share the gospel in Christ's way without humiliating people of other faiths' (my italics).[9]

In line with its ecumenical agenda the Lausanne Movement promotes the concept of 'unity in love'. *The Cape Town Commitment – A Confession of Faith and a Call to Action,* declares that love calls for unity. The command of Jesus 'that his disciples should love one another is linked to his prayer that they should be one. Both the command and the prayer are missional – "that the world may know you are my disciples"... We urgently seek a new global partnership within the body of Christ across all continents, rooted in profound mutual love, mutual submission, and dramatic economic sharing without paternalism or unhealthy dependency.'[10]

Vatican's ecumenical movement

The modern ecumenical movement, to which Lausanne is deeply committed, emerged from the Second Vatican Council (1962-65). In his opening speech, Pope John XXIII admitted that past efforts to achieve unity through force of arms had failed. So the Pontiff announced a different approach. He said that the Catholic Church, 'raising the torch of religious truth by means of this Ecumenical Council, desires to show herself to be the loving mother of all, benign, full of mercy and goodness towards the brethren who are separated from her.'[11]

The Vatican's Decree on Ecumenism declared the restoration of unity among all Christians to be one of the principal concerns of the Pope. 'Christ the Lord founded one Church and one Church only. However, many Christian communions present themselves to men as the true inheritors of Jesus Christ; all indeed profess to be followers of the Lord but differ in mind and go their different ways, as if Christ Himself were divided. Such division openly contradicts the will of Christ, scandalizes the world, and damages the holy cause of preaching the Gospel to every creature.'[12]

According to the Vatican, Christ has been rousing divided Christians to remorse over their divisions and to a longing for unity. 'Everywhere large numbers have felt the impulse of this grace, and among our separated brethren also there increases from day to day the movement, fostered by the grace of the Holy Spirit, for the restoration of unity among all Christians. This movement toward unity is called ecumenical.'[13] It is a movement that strives to overcome the obstacles that have caused disunity in the Church. 'But even in spite of them it remains true that all who have been justified by faith in Baptism are members of Christ's body, and have a right to be called Christian, and so are correctly accepted as brothers by the children of the Catholic Church.'[14]

Those referred to by the Vatican as 'separated brethren', whether considered as individuals or as communities and churches, are not blessed with that unity which Jesus Christ wished to bestow on them, for it is only through Christ's Catholic Church 'that they can benefit fully from the means of salvation. We believe that Our Lord entrusted all the blessings of the New Covenant to the apostolic college alone, of which Peter is the head, in order to establish the one Body of Christ on earth to which all should be fully incorporated who belong in any way to the people of God.'[15]

The purpose of the ecumenical movement is to initiate plans and activities that promote Christian unity. 'When the obstacles to perfect ecclesiastical communion have been gradually overcome, all Christians will at last, in a common celebration of the Eucharist, be gathered into the one and only Church in that unity which Christ bestowed on His Church from the beginning. We believe that this unity subsists in the Catholic Church as something she can never lose, and we hope that it will continue to increase until the end of time.'[16]

Since 1962 successive popes have made the ecumenical movement a top priority in their quest to persuade all Christians to worship according to their rules. The ultimate goal of the ecumenical movement is to bring all churches into full, visible, sacramental unity around the Roman Catholic Eucharist.

The Catholic-Evangelical Accord signed in 1994 by leading evangelicals and Roman Catholics is a product of the ecumenical movement. The Accord calls on both groups to embrace each other as fellow Christians and ends with these words: 'We do know that this is a time of opportunity—and, if of opportunity, then of responsibility—for Evangelicals and Catholics to be Christians together in a way that helps prepare the world for the coming of Him to whom belongs the kingdom, the power, and the glory forever. Amen.' In his booklet, *Reversing the Reformation, The Catholic/Evangelical Accord Examined* (1994), American Pastor Gil Rugh says that the evangelicals who signed this document, in a sense, are apologising for the Protestant Reformation and all that it stood for. He explains that the Accord makes light of the heavy price the Reformers had to pay as they fought for the pure Gospel.[17] 'With one blanket statement, one billion Catholics have all been declared Christians. The Roman Catholic Church has given up nothing. But Evangelicals have abandoned historic Christianity.'[18] He concludes: 'It is my fear though, that what we see going on with this accord is not promoting true, biblical unity. True unity must be based on the truth of God's Word or else it is a false unity.'[19]

Pope John Paul II in 2000 made his view crystal clear that ecumenical unity is 'concretely embodied in the Catholic Church, despite the human limitations of her members, and it is at work in varying degrees in all the elements of holiness and truth to be found in the other Churches and Ecclesial Communities. As gifts properly belonging to the Church of Christ, these elements lead them continuously towards full unity.'[20]

We have seen that the two key founders of the Lausanne Movement, Billy Graham and John Stott, were both committed to the ecumenical movement in the full knowledge of Vatican plans to draw all so-called 'separated' churches back into the flock of Rome. The vision of the Pope is that 'all Christians will at last, in a common celebration of the Eucharist, be gathered into the one and only Church'.[21]

Following the euphoria of the Cape Town Congress, Douglas Birdsall made the ecumenical ambitions of the Lausanne Movement plain and obvious. Looking forward to the next Lausanne Congress, he wrote in a memo published in *Lausanne World Pulse* (December 2010): 'It is my hope in 2020 that the evangelical Church will make progress in its relationships with the historic churches of the Christian faith. It is in this same spirit of humility and integrity that we must extend the hand of fellowship to the Catholic, Orthodox, and Ecumenical Church. We must embrace those in renewal movements, such as the Pentecostal, Charismatic, and Emergent. It is only in community with the churches of the past and of the present and future that the Church as a whole can move forward as a powerful witness in the world.'[22]

So there is no longer any doubt where Lausanne is going. Its long-term aim is to take 'separated' evangelicals back to the mother church of Rome. And along the way it will eagerly promote the ideas of the emerging church. In effect, Lausanne has declared war on the Reformation and the reformed faith. For all its spectacular choreography and eloquent presentations, Cape Town 2010 looks like error masquerading as Christian zeal, even if true believers are caught up in the excitement.

True unity and the false unity of ecumenism

Scripture teaches that true believers, those who are justified by faith in Christ alone and sealed by the Holy Spirit, are one in Christ. Therefore true believers are like-minded, for they have the same mind of Christ, the same Spirit, the same Word of truth and preach the same Gospel of salvation. True believers rejoice in the truth of God's Word, and contend for the truth of the Gospel. God promises his people that he will be their God in truth and in righteousness (Zechariah 8.8). So the unity of God's 'called-out' and set apart people (*saints*) is a spiritual union, for all are joined together as members of the Body of Christ. The invisible Church of Jesus Christ is truly united, for there is 'one Lord, one faith, one baptism' (Ephesians 4.5).

While ecumenism claims to unite the Church in love, it is indifferent to doctrinal truth. But Scripture teaches that genuine love rejoices in the truth (3 John 3-4). It follows that the 'love' that unites Lausanne is counterfeit, for it is 'love' that does not rejoice in doctrinal truth. The prophet Isaiah describes the idolatrous treachery of Israel, 'which swear by the name of the Lord, and make mention of the God of Israel, but not in truth, nor in righteousness' (Isaiah 48.1). In like manner, the ecumenical movement swears by the name of Christ, yet does not do so in truth and righteousness, but in counterfeit love.

Included around the ecumenical table are those who do not believe in the fundamentals of the Christian faith. The false unity of the ecumenical movement undermines the Gospel of truth, for it mixes truth and error. It leads to confusion, for there is no agreement on doctrinal truth and what the Gospel is, how it should be preached, and no agreement on how God is to be worshipped. The mantra of ecumenism, 'love calls for unity', opens the door wide to false teachers.

In view of the ecumenical nature of the Lausanne Movement, we need to be reminded of the danger of false teaching, a theme that runs through the New Testament. The apostle Paul warned the elders of the church in Ephesus that after his departure savage wolves would come among them. And these savage wolves, these false teachers, speaking perverse things to draw away disciples, would arise from *within* the Church (Acts 20.29-30). The apostle warned the churches of Galatia of false teachers who would pervert the Gospel of Christ (Galatians 1.7). He warned the Corinthian church of those who preach another 'Jesus' and another 'gospel'. He called them false apostles who disguise themselves as servants of righteousness, as apostles of Christ, just as Satan disguises himself as an angel of light (2 Corinthians 11.13-15). The warning is clear—the threat of false teachers is ever present, and so the Gospel of truth must be defended against the ministers of Satan. The Church must do all it can to expose and oppose false teaching. False teachers must be identified and put out of the Church.

What are the fruits of a movement that claims to be 'united in love', but that has little interest in sound doctrine? Can such a movement contend for the Gospel of truth once for all delivered to the saints? Does Lausanne oppose false teaching wherever it is found, or, in its ecumenical zeal, has it turned a blind eye to many heretical doctrines?

(Endnotes)

1 Fuller Theological Seminary website, News, 'Fuller Hosts Global Conversation on Pasadena Campus', April 2010

2 Lausanne Movement website, Gatherings, Cape Town 2010, Endorsements, 'What Global Leaders Were Saying About Cape Town 2010', Rick Warren

3 Youtube, Rick Warren on Cape Town 2010, http://www.youtube.com/watch?v=w-8pAArC Zc0&list=PL867F5110AFBE126B&index=1&feature=plpp_video

4 Lausanne Movement website, Gatherings, Cape Town 2010, Endorsements, 'What Global Leaders Were Saying About Cape Town 2010', John Stott

5 Cape Town 2010 Congress website, Cape Town participants' qualifications. 'Characteristics of each Cape Town 2010 participant should include'

6 Brehm Center website, http://www.brehmcenter.com/loves/art_and_faith/

7 Brehm Center website, http://www.brehmcenter.com/education/brehm_emphasis/

8 Lausanne Movement website, One year later, Reconciled in Christ: A Behind-the-Scenes look at the development of the Cape Town 2010 Opening/Closing Ceremony Music CD

9 World Council of Churches website, Greetings to the 3rd Lausanne Congress for World Evangelization, Cape Town, South Africa, Sunday 17 October 2010, By the Rev Dr Olav Fykse Tveit, general secretary of the World Council of Churches, 'All this is from God': Mission as Ministry of Reconciliation

10 The Lausanne Movement website, The Cape Town Commitment – A Confession of Faith and a Call to Action, 2011, Part 1, Paragraph 9, 'We love the people of God'

11 Second Vatican Council – 1962-1965, Pope John's Opening Speech to the Council, October 11, 1962, the first day of the Council. Pope John delivered this address in St. Peter's Basilica.

12 Second Vatican Council, Decree on Ecumenism, Proclaimed By His Holiness, Pope Paul VI on November 21, 1964, Introduction, paragraph 1

13 Ibid. Introduction, paragraph 1

14 Ibid. Chapter 1, Catholic principles on Ecumenism, paragraph 3,

15 Ibid.

16 Ibid. paragraph 4

17 Gil Rugh, *Reversing the Reformation, The Catholic/Evangelical Accord Examined*, Indian Hills Community Church, 1994, p28

18 Ibid. p31

19 Ibid. p4

20 Pope John Paul II to the Bishops, Clergy and Lay Faithful at the close of the Great Jubilee of the Year 2000, Part 4, Witness to love, Ecumenical commitment, paragraph 48

21 Reference 16

22 *Lausanne World Pulse*, December 2010, 'Pressing on towards 2020 in Humility, Reflection, and Hope' by Douglas Birdsall, http://www.lausanneworldpulse.com/pdf/issues/December2010PDF2.pdf

Chapter 5

Promoting the arts and the emerging church

The Cape Town Congress was characterised by visual images and a large number of dramas performed by the Lausanne arts team. The stated aim of the Congress was 'to carry out the vision for an arts presence that will enrich our time together, strengthen the communication of the congress themes and mark the importance of the arts for the missional task. We have a unique opportunity to celebrate the arts across a wide spectrum of culture diversity.'[1] Most of the plenary sessions had dramatic presentations, some of which are described below.

Dr Tim Keller of Redeemer Presbyterian Church, New York, in his talk 'God's Global Urban Mission – Contextualization', asserted that churches which are 'contextualised' for the city have to be extremely culturally sensitive, and this means that they must pay particular attention to the arts. 'In most churches artists, musicians and visual artists are hired hands. We have things that we want to do and then we hire artists and we ask them to do it. But in cities the artists are kind of an ethnic group. They have their own culture. They have their own way of thinking about things. To have an artist-friendly church the artist must be empowered. The arts have to be taken very, very seriously.'[2]

Lausanne redeems the arts

The report, *Redeeming the Arts* (2005), produced by Lausanne Issue Group 17, explains why the arts are so important to the Church. We are reminded that in the Western Church, prior to the Reformation, 'visual art played a central role in the liturgy and devotional life of the church. Cathedrals, abbeys, and parish churches were adorned inside and out with frescoes, sculptures, and stained glass, while the utmost craftsmanship and valuable materials were lavished upon liturgical implements.'[3]

However, the Protestant Reformation of the sixteenth century ushered in a new era. 'Theologians such as John Calvin contended that any use of images in worship would lead to idolatry—though the gift of artistry in other contexts was still viewed as God-given and so to be accepted and appreciated. The Protestant Reformation thus turned to emphasizing the word as central for the worshiping community, all but eliminating the visual arts.'[4]

Redeeming the Arts says that as a consequence of the Reformation, 'the majority within faith communities simply neglected the arts, having no understanding and receiving no teaching about the place of the arts in the life of faith.'[5] The report asserts that the task of global evangelism is a task of communication. 'It is evident that art, too, is about communication. The way in which art communicates is of course unique to the medium, but the power of the arts to move us, engage us, and help us to see with fresh eyes is indisputable.'[6] And more: 'Imagination has been neglected as a resource for helping us to think more clearly about the world. As a result, we have impoverished Christian thinking and understanding. The time has come for Christians to recover the imagination and to discern its value for faith and life... There is a need for a paradigm shift in how we view the arts—a fresh vision to help us understand how the recovery of the imagination and the affirmation of the gift of artistic creativity can be both celebrative and significant for the church.'[7]

While acknowledging that only Christ can transform the human condition, *Redeeming the Arts* says: 'We can show that the arts allow for diversity as they "witness" in verbal and nonverbal ways to the truth about the human condition... They can also draw people to Christ when linked to acts of compassion and service. The arts enable cross-cultural and cross-generational communication and contextualization. Social and economic barriers can be overcome through collaborative art making, and arts used in therapies can invigorate health and healing.'[8]

Another perceived benefit is that art can enhance the worship of a community. 'Art can capture things for us where words alone fail. Art can both remind us of what we have forgotten and help us to see what we have never understood. It is time for the church to employ all of the arts in worship so that they might do their work and give glimpses of truth, beauty, and glory. When we have rehearsed our story, we are renewed and empowered to live out that story in conformity with the beauty of the image of Christ.'[9]

In *Redeeming the Arts* we see a fundamental difference in the position of the Church of Rome and the Reformers. Roman Catholicism has always promoted the use of images, icons, pictures and other works of art in the 'worship' of God. The Reformed faith, in obedience to the Second Commandment, removed images, icons and works of art from the Church in order to focus on preaching, teaching, and understanding the Word of God. What is significant is that Lausanne's position on the arts is entirely consistent with that of the Roman Catholic Church, and entirely at odds with that of the Reformation.

Defining the emerging church

To help us interpret Lausanne's enthusiasm for the arts we need to turn to the so-called 'emerging church' movement. But first we need a word of explanation, for many people have difficulty in understanding the emerging church, and this is because it is an amorphous movement that is difficult to define.

The emerging church has *emerged* among church leaders with a postmodern mindset, who believe that traditional Christianity has failed. As there is no such thing as absolute truth in postmodern thinking, no one can be sure that they really understand the Gospel. In an interview with *Christianity Today*, Brian McLaren, an elder spokesman for the emerging church, explained: 'I don't think we've got the gospel right yet. What does it mean to be "saved"? When I read the Bible, I don't see it meaning, "I'm going to heaven after I die." Before modern evangelicalism nobody accepted Jesus Christ as their personal Saviour, or walked down an aisle, or said the sinner's prayer.'[10]

McLaren says elsewhere that he has been involved in an interesting and profoundly enjoyable conversation for the last ten years or so. 'It's a conversation about what it means to be a "new kind of Christian"—not an angry and reactionary fundamentalist, not a stuffy traditionalist… not an overly enthused Bible-waving fanatic—but something fresh and authentic and challenging and adventurous. Around the world, millions of people have gotten involved in this conversation.'[11] He is concerned that for many people the name 'Jesus' has become a symbol of exclusion, as if Jesus' statement, 'I am the way, and of the truth, and the life; no one comes to the Father except through me' actually means, 'I am in the way of people seeking truth and life. I won't let anyone get to God unless he comes through me.'[12] McLaren asserts that in the Bible salvation emphatically does not mean 'save from hell' or 'give eternal life after death', as many preachers seem to imply in sermon after sermon. 'Rather its meaning varies from passage to passage, but in general, in any context, save means "get out of trouble". The trouble could be sickness, war, political intrigue, oppression, poverty, imprisonment, or any kind of danger or evil.'[13]

And so adherents of the emerging church (*emergents*) are engaged in an on-going, never-ending *conversation* in an effort to see the Gospel in a new way. An article in *Lausanne World Pulse* says that Brian McLaren has correctly warned that contemporary Christians need to radically rethink their understanding and practice of evangelism.[14] McLaren argues that we need to recognise that we may not fully understand the good news of the Gospel, and therefore we need to rediscover it. We need to understand that the Gospel is not first of all 'information on how one goes to heaven after death... but rather a vision of what life can be in all its dimensions' and a way of life to bring that vision into reality.[15] McLaren urges Christians to redefine their understanding of discipleship, bearing in mind that evangelism is not about recruiting refugees from earth to heaven, but recruiting revolutionaries who are willing to compassionately 'bring the good and healing will of heaven to earth in all its crises'.[16]

Emergents want a new kind of Christianity that places stories over doctrine—a religion that focuses on experience and feelings. They believe the Bible should be interpreted through the lens of the culture. They want a new kind of worship that promotes all the arts; that uses images and dance, candles and PowerPoint presentations to enhance their worship experience. They believe that faith is about the here and now, and so they typically support social initiatives, and are especially concerned about the environment and global warming. They want the Church to be seeker-friendly, a place where unbelievers, whom they call 'seekers', feel at home.

As we shall see in this study, the Lausanne Movement, which was founded on the compromised principles of new evangelicalism, is currently on the same theological path that the emerging church has been following for the last few decades with respect to ecumenism, the social gospel, the threat of global warming, the global conversation, the importance of storytelling the Gospel, and the promotion of the arts in worship.

Arts in the emerging church

Central to the emerging church is the belief that images should take precedence over words. An ordained Anglican priest who works with the Archbishop of Canterbury's Fresh Expressions team, Ian Modsby, explains: 'We are now very much a visual culture, which creates real opportunities for engagement through a metaphorical approach. It is in this ancient, refreshed approach, that the Emerging Church seeks to enable spiritual encounter through the imagination. This is nothing new. The prophets used the arts and music to enable people to imagine another way of being through an artistic approach. It is in this playful way that the Emerging Church mixes up the secular and spiritual – through arts events on a theme of the spiritual.'[17]

In his book *The Emerging Church* (2003), Dan Kimball says that more and more pastors and leaders from the emerging church movement are actually into the arts. He writes: 'I have been hearing how emerging churches are incorporating paintings in their preaching as illustrations. Some churches even allow artists to paint during the worship time as an expression of worship.'[18] Kimball asserts that since emerging church culture highly values the arts it should embrace and encourage artists and art enthusiasts. As a consequence more and more artists are joining emerging church communities. 'When we design worship gatherings, we look for ways to incorporate the arts. One of the ways we do this is to use art consistently in all of our PowerPoint presentations during the musical worship, teaching, and prayer meditations.'[19]

Brian McLaren shared his thoughts at the annual Willow Creek Arts Conference (2008). He declared that the arts have an incredibly important role in the Church. He says it's exciting to see dance, poetry, the spoken word, drama and film-making being brought into the worship life of the Church. 'But what I'm really excited about is the next step when the arts are used to improve, and humanize and deepen the churches' commitment to the world. In other words, we can use the arts to enrich the Church, but then if the Church doesn't turn outwards to have some impact on the world at large, I think it becomes like the Dead Sea where everything comes in and nothing goes out. So the artists [must] start to think not just how do we deepen the Church, but how do we equip the Church for a greater engagement with the world.'[20]

Promoting drama in Cape Town

Following the pattern of the emerging church, the Lausanne Movement made sure that the arts, drama and visual images had a significant presence at the Cape Town Congress. 'Art in all of its forms serves as a means of communication, opening us to fresh perspectives and allowing us to make discoveries about ourselves, our world and the God who has created all things. Art is able to bridge our differences and cross cultural barriers. It can also provide a way into exploring the deep and important human questions – which are ultimately religious questions... Our desire is that the presence of the arts at the historic Cape Town 2010 gathering will be seen as expressions of praise to the God that we serve.'[21] *The Cape Town Commitment* made the remarkable statement: 'Artists at their best are truth-tellers and so the arts constitute one important way in which we can speak the truth of the gospel. Drama, dance, story, music and visual image can be expressions both of the reality of our brokenness, and of the hope that is centred in the gospel that all things will be made new.'[22]

The above statement about the 'truth of the gospel' is completely false, and deeply heretical, for spiritual truth is found in Scripture alone, and not in drama, dance or music. It is God's Word, recorded in Scripture, that declares God's truth. Our Lord said, 'Sanctify them by Your truth. Your word is truth' (John 17.17). The Protestant reformed faith believes that Sciputre is the final authority and inerrant source of all spiritual truth.

Paul's letter to the Ephesians

A drama performed on the Lausanne stage prepares the audience for the biblical exposition of Ephesians 1. The scene is of a group of believers anxiously awaiting the arrival of Tychicus, who is carrying Paul's letter. When he does not arrive on time, the group is fearful that

Drama at Lausanne: Letter to Ephesians

The scene is of a group of believers anxiously awaiting the arrival of Tychicus, who is carrying Paul's letter to the Ephesians.

One of the group reminds the others that 'Tye' is not exactly punctual, indeed, he's always late.

The conversation then turns to the Roman Empire, which is described as similar to dealing with a swarm of bees.

Tychicus triumphantly produces Paul's letter from his sock, with the crack: 'The soldiers don't check socks'.

he has been arrested at a Roman checkpoint. But there is another possible explanation. One of the group reminds the others that 'Tye' is not exactly punctual, indeed, he's always late. But the reputation of Tychicus is being falsely impugned, for the apostle Paul refers to him as a beloved brother, faithful minister and fellow servant in the Lord (Ephesians 6.21 and Colossians 4.7).

The conversation then turns to the Roman Empire, which is described as similar to dealing with a swarm of bees, for when they turn on you, then you get stung. One of the group comments: 'Maybe there will be something in that letter about what to do with bees.' Eventually Tychicus arrives explaining that he had to go through two Roman checkpoints. And then the punchline of the drama—to the surprise of the gathering, Tychicus triumphantly produces Paul's letter from his sock with the crack: 'The soldiers don't check socks'.[23] The audience laughs, for they have been entertained. But this facile drama does nothing to improve their understanding of God's Word; indeed, it has trivialised God's Word.

Reconciliation

A dramatic presentation, entitled 'South Africa in Process', provides an example of what Lausanne means by reconciliation. The drama starts with two armed men, a black comrade and a white settler, who are at total war—no mercy, no love, no hesitation; the simple aim is one bullet for one settler, one bullet for one terrorist. The scene changes to a white woman kneeling in prayer: 'By grace you save us, O God, through faith. We know this is not our own doing but yours. Our lives are your workmanship, not ours. Jesus bring your peace near, bring us through the dividing wall of hostility, into one household with you. Make us into one whole, joined together, holy. By grace you save, O God.' In response to this prayer the two men lay down their guns and the audience applauds.[24] But what is the message of this drama? Does it declare 'the truth of the gospel'? Do the audience now understand that sinners are reconciled to God through the Cross of Christ (2 Corithians 5.18-21)?

The pantomime of Ephesians 2

This pantomime is indicative of the spirit of Lausanne. The performance is explained as follows: 'A team of dancers pantomime the

Drama at Laussane: Reconciliation

The drama starts with two armed men, a black comrade and a white settler

The scene changes to a white woman kneeling in prayer:

'Jesus bring your peace near, bring us through the dividing wall of hostility, into one household with you.'

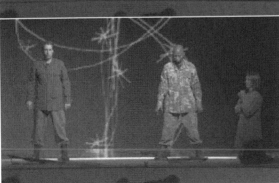

In response to this prayer the two men lay down their guns and the audience applauds

Pantomime of Ephesians 2

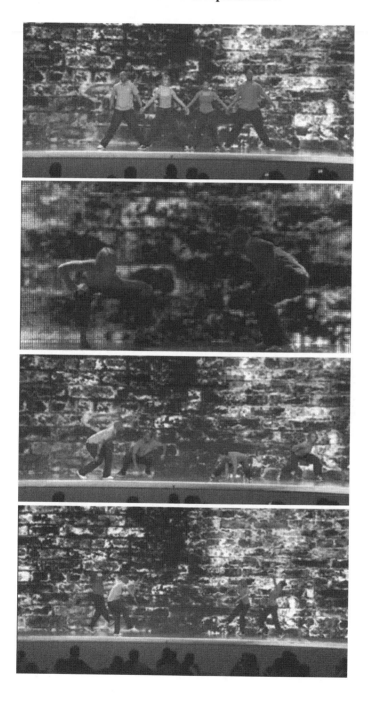

theme of Ephesians 2, illustrating that Christ has broken down the dividing wall of hostility.' Choreography was by the Cape Town 2010 performing arts team. The music credit was 'Dirty Pool' by Audio-Sparx, a huge digital audio market-place which advertises itself as the music that powers Hollywood. 'Dirty Pool' is described as 'dreamy and bizarre dramatic background cue with hip-hop elements reflecting the dark and dangerous side of urban life'. The performance comprises four dancers prancing around the Lausanne stage, performing a series of moves—jumping, shaking, rolling, flinging their arms about, to the beat of 'Dirty Pool'.[25]

This bizarre pantomine at a plenary gathering of the Congress really speaks volumes about the Lausanne Movement and its commitment to the arts. The leaders of Lausanne apparently believe that the 'dark and dangerous' audio sound of 'Dirty Pool' is helpful in worshipping God. They apparently feel that this performance helps them to have a better understanding of Ephesians 2. But of one thing we can be sure, the Holy God of Heaven is not worshipped by the sounds of 'Dirty Pool'. Nothing that is 'dark and dangerous' will come into the presence of the God of Scripture, who lives in unapproachable light (1 Timothy 6.16).

Lausanne's commitment to the visual arts is a clear indication that it is following the ways and methods of the emerging church movement. Yet it is difficult to understand how four thousand intelligent Christian men and women could witness these trite performances and actually believe that the Body of Christ was being edified. But is seems that the music which powers Hollywood is the music that appeals to the Lausanne gathering. And here we see the tragedy of compromise— while Lausanne uses drama, visual images and music to cultivate the imagination, it has little place for biblical truth, as will become clear in the following chapters.

(Endnotes)

1   The Lausanne Movement website, Cape Town 2010, Arts at Cape Town 2010

2   Cape Town 2010 website, cited from Tim Keller's talk, 'God's Global Urban Mission – Contextualization', http://www.lausanne.org/cape-town-2010/schedule.html

3 Lausanne Occasional Paper No.46, Redeeming the Arts, Produced by the Issue Group on this topic at the 2004 Forum for World Evangelization hosted by the Lausanne Committee for World Evangelization, Art, the Church, and the Imagination, A Long and Complex History, p12

4 Ibid.

5 Ibid.

6 Ibid. Prologue, p8

7 Ibid. Prologue, Education, p8

8 Ibid. Prologue, Transformation, p9

9 Ibid. The Arts and Worship, p26

10 *Christianity Today*, 'The Emergent Mystique', November 2004

11 Brian McLaren, *Everything must change: Jesus, global crisis, and a revolution of hope*, Thomas Nelson, 2007, p3

12 Brian McLaren, *A Generous Orthodoxy*, Grand Rapids, Zondervan, 2004, p70

13 Ibid. p93

14 *Lausanne World Pulse*, 'The Culture of Peace and Evangelism' by Paulus Widjaja, October 2007

15 Brian McLaren, 'A Radical Rethinking of Our Evangelistic Strategy', 2004, Theology, News & Notes. Fall: 4-6, 22

16 Ibid.

17 Iain Mobsby Blog, Anglimergent, emerging church & arts-as-mission, February 2008, http://anglimergent.ning.com/profiles/blogs/1972049:BlogPost:9883

18 Dan Kimball, *The Emerging Church*, Zondervan, 2003, p147

19 Ibid. p148

20 Brian McLaren shares some thoughts after session three of 'Arise', the 2008 Willow Creek Arts Conference, Youtube video, http://www.youtube.com/watch?v=nVMH82Xwnj0

21 Cape Town 2010 website, Arts at Cape Town 2010

22 Lausanne Movement website, The Cape Town Commitment, Part 2, Section IIA, 'Truth and the arts in mission'

23 Cape Town 2010 website, Video, Bible Exposition: Drama 'Letter', http://conversation.lausanne.org/en/conversations/detail/11331

24 Ibid. Video, Reconciliation - Drama 'Our Boys On the Border', http://conversation.lausanne.org/en/conversations/detail/11419

25 Ibid. Video, Bible Exposition: Dance 'Reach', http://conversation.lausanne.org/en/conversations/detail/11552

Chapter 6

The orality movement

We now come to the high point of the third Lausanne gathering on world evangelization. The Cape Town Congress is told that storytelling is the modern method by which the whole Church is to take the whole Gospel to the whole world. The session entitled, 'Communicating to Oral Learners', described the concept of storytelling (also known as the orality movement) as a breakthrough strategy for spreading the Gospel.[1] Dr Grant Lovejoy, Professor of Preaching at Southwestern Baptist Theological Seminary, told the Congress that there are over four billion oral learners in the world—one billion out of necessity because they are illiterate, and three billion from choice, for they prefer not to read, and therefore are known as 'preferenced oral learners'. He argued that the Church needed to change the traditional way of taking the Gospel to unreached people. Christians should develop new appropriate methods of communication, such as storytelling, drama, songs, visual arts, poetry, chants and music, for they are the most effective methods for reaching the four billion oral learners of this world with the Gospel of Christ.[2]

In an advance paper for the Congress, Grant Lovejoy writes that Jesus knew the value of parables, but he 'also used other kinds of stories, object lessons, miracles, and his own example to teach. In these and other ways Jesus demonstrated himself to be an audience-sensitive communicator.'[3] He says that 'using appropriate oral strategies with oral learners leads to better understanding and acceptance of the Gospel. It contributes to better discipleship. Oral methods are essential in equipping oral learners as leaders in their culture.'[4] He claims that before writing was invented, everyone lived by spoken communication, thus by orality. He acknowledges that the authority for this assertion is the scholar Walter Ong, who 'called such groups primary oral cultures and called their way of communicating primary orality'.[5] We learn more about Walter Ong in the next chapter.

Beginnings of the orality movement

The orality movement had small beginnings with a missionary couple serving in Papua New Guinea. They used a chronological Bible teaching method, telling the Bible story from Creation to Christ. Interest in the concept of orality developed during the 1980s, as missionaries serving with the Foreign Mission Board (now the International Mission Board – IMB) of the Southern Baptist Convention in the Philippines, came to the conclusion that existing approaches to Bible presentation were too literate. They believed chronological Bible 'storying' that utilised storytelling followed by dialogue was the way forward.[6]

During the 1990s the concept of storytelling was accepted by many missionary organisations. In the article, 'Storytelling the Gospel: The Way Forward', Jim Bowman, director of Scriptures in Use (SIU) – an organisation that specialises in training grassroots church planters – writes that among traditional oral cultures storytelling forms the very basis of their understanding of truth.[7]

Orality issue group

In 2004 the Lausanne Committee on World Evangelization claimed to have been led by the Holy Spirit to hold a conference to deal with the most significant issues in the task of taking the Gospel to the world. The theme of the conference, held in Thailand, was 'A new vision, a new heart, a renewed call'. Over a thousand participants from 130 countries were involved in the 31 Issue Groups. Even before the conference Lausanne's global research programme had identified oral methods of communication as an important issue facing the Church. And so the Orality Issue Group was given the task of answering Marcus Vegh's question: 'How do you make disciples of oral learners?' (page 14). The Group concluded that missionary initiatives of previous centuries had failed to engage with 'people groups' made up of oral learners, and therefore a new approach was needed. They believed that storytelling was the most effective method for taking the Gospel to 'oral learners'.

Key organisations represented on the Orality Group were the International Mission Board of the Southern Baptist Convention, Campus Crusade for Christ, Wycliffe Bible Translators, Southern Baptist Theological Seminary, FEBA Radio, Trans-World Radio (TWR), Serving in Mission and Scripture in Use, among others. The work of the Orality Group resulted in this affirmation: 'We acknowledge the reality that much of the world is made up of oral learners who understand best when information comes to them by means of stories. A large proportion of the world's populations are either unable to or unwilling to absorb information through written communications. Therefore, a need exists to share the "Good News" and to disciple new Christians in story form and parables.'[8]

Another outcome of the Orality Group was the booklet *Making Disciples of Oral Learners* (2005). The booklet's editorial committee included Professor Grant Lovejoy as chairman, and Rev Avery Willis, vice-president of the International Mission Board of the Southern Baptist Convention, as convener of the group. *Making Disciples* is regarded as so important that it has been translated into Korean, Chinese, French, Russian, Spanish and Arabic.

Literate styles cause confusion

A theme that runs through *Making Disciples of Oral Learners* is that a literate approach to communicating the Gospel is ineffective among those who live in an oral culture. Two examples illustrate the problem. The first is that of an Indian pastor who shared the good news of the Gospel in his village, but to his surprise people were not able to understand the message. He continued to preach the Gospel, but there were few results. He concluded that the problem was that he used 'a lecture method with printed books' which he learnt in Bible school.[9] He decided that people were not hearing the Gospel because it was being communicated by 'literate means'.

Making Disciples interprets this example as demonstrating that highly literate communication styles that 'use the printed page or expositional, analytical and logical presentations of God's word' make it almost impossible for oral learners to understand the message of the Gospel.[10] This is because 'oral learners find it difficult to follow literate-styled presentations, even if they are made orally. It is not enough to take materials created for literates and simply read them onto a recorded format. Making something audible does not necessarily make it an "oral" style of communication.'[11] The implication is that teaching materials with literate stylistic features are likely to confuse oral learners. Indeed, oral learners 'cannot or will not learn well through print-based instruction'.[12] So in the eyes of the Orality Group it is pointless to use the printed Word of God to instruct oral learners.

The Orality Group provides as the second example a church-planter from North India, who as a young man committed his life to the Lord and was baptized. Later he had the opportunity to study in a Bible college where he learned the Word of God: 'There I was taught in the Western-style of education. When I came back from the college I used the same Western methods to preach the Gospel but nobody accepted Christ. I became very discouraged and I was thinking I would leave the ministry.' Then he got the opportunity to attend a training seminar where he learned how to plant churches among illiterate people by storytelling the Gospel. 'I was greatly influenced by the training. I returned to my mission field and used those same methods. Storytelling changed my ministry. So many people believed on Jesus Christ and were baptized.'[13]

These two examples are used to support the assertion that using the written Word of God to preach the Gospel to oral learners is ineffective and likely to cause confusion. Indeed, it can even be counter-productive to quote printed Bible verses, for oral learners do not react well to print-based instruction.

The Orality Group claimed that to make disciples of oral learners it is necessary to use 'communication forms that are familiar within the culture: stories, proverbs, drama, songs, chants, and poetry. Literate approaches rely on lists, outlines, word studies, apologetics, and theological jargon. These literate methods are largely ineffective among two-thirds of the world's peoples.'[14] The assertion that a literate approach, which makes use of the written Word to preach the Gospel of Christ, is ineffective among two-thirds of the world's people is contrary to Scripture, for God has promised that his Word will not return to him void (Isaiah 55.11).

Jesus the master storyteller

The orality movement presents a parody of the Lord Jesus as a master storyteller. We are told that 'Jesus was a storyteller, yet the church has largely ignored or forgotten his communication policies. The belief in the superiority of the written page has been deeply engrained into the Western mind.'[15] While the assertion that the Lord Jesus taught by stories and parables is true, it is not the whole truth, for he also taught from the Scriptures. He started his ministry by reading from the book of Isaiah. When he taught on marriage and divorce he referred to the book of Genesis. In his Sermon on the Mount, he quoted from the Law of Moses. So the teaching of the Lord cannot be contained in stories alone, for he taught about the character of God, the sinful nature of man, God's hatred of sin and evil, the reality of hell, the truth of God's Word, the need for repentance and the forgiveness of sin through his death on the Cross, the hope of the resurrection and final judgement. He taught about the coming judgement and the wrath of God against all sin and wickedness. Indeed, the Lord taught a nation (Israel) that was founded and nurtured on a *book*. He himself was the divine author of that *book*, the very *book* that he himself read and meditated on as the Son of Man, the *book* that spoke of him.

Oral Bible

The orality movement claims to have developed what it has chosen to call an oral Bible that 'allows God's Word to be produced accurately from memory for the purpose of re-telling. The "oral Bible" is the singular key to unlocking church planting movements among unreached people groups. However, that "oral Bible" must penetrate the people group to its worldview level belief system. Only then will a Bible become meaningful and useful. The only Bible that will be effective during the lifetime of the vast majority of unreached people is an "oral Bible", probably best presented in narrative form.'[16]

So what exactly is an oral Bible? While *Making Disciples* concedes that there is no definitive oral Bible, it provides a working definition of an oral Bible as 'the accumulated Bible stories that have been told to an oral society'. Typically, this is between 50 and 225 stories. 'These are usually told in chronological order, though not always, since many times specific problems, concerns, fears etc. may need to be addressed first. So an oral Bible may differ to some extent from one culture to another, depending on felt and/or actual needs, worldview, theology and so forth. Those stories which form the cornerstone of Christian faith will be represented in virtually all oral Bible collections... An oral Bible becomes the permanent possession of an oral communicator and is available for use at all times. Oral communicators are able to retain, recall, and repeat from memory their oral Bible.'[17]

Story Runners, a project of Campus Crusade, says that 'oral cultures use their Story Bibles just like we literates use our written Bibles... Because a Story Bible is the Word of God, it is useful for teaching, rebuking, correcting and training in righteousness (2 Tim 3:16). Missions and churches can use Story Bibles for evangelism, discipleship and leadership training. Story Bibles dwell primarily in the hearts and minds of storytellers who have internalized the stories and can tell them from memory, but they can also spread through media. As more people hear and learn the stories, the Story Bible becomes embedded into the fabric of the people group's culture. As a result, people follow Jesus, and churches are planted.'[18]

There is no definitive oral Bible. This means that each teacher and each disciple has their own version of an oral Bible. Moreover, an individual's oral Bible will change over time as their memory fades. Clearly, an oral Bible does not endure forever, as God's Word does, but only as long as an individual's unreliable memory endures. The deep irony of the oral Bible is that it is the product of highly literate intellectuals, who promote their concept of 'orality' through literate means, such as books, journal articles, theological papers and PowerPoint presentations.

Crafting Bible stories

The oral Bible is created by crafting stories. *Making Disciples* explains: 'Crafting Bible stories is shaping the stories from a literature format to an oral format and *making such changes as needed* to maintain a clear focus on the story's main point(s), to give clarity in telling, and *to make necessary changes needed for accommodating certain worldview issues* and story continuity leading to the storying track objective of evangelism, discipling, leader training, etc'[19] (my italics).

Making Disciples says that a storytelling approach involves selecting and crafting stories that convey the essential biblical message in a way that is sensitive to the worldview of the receptor society. 'Unbelievers need Christians to provide His Word in culturally appropriate formats in order for them to understand it and respond to it... those who respond need to be able to reproduce it—to share it themselves with others who can, in turn, share it with others, with this pattern being repeated many times over. A spiritual movement of this sort can provide a foundation for faith, witness, and church life.'[20]

The orality movement declares that an assortment of self-selected crafted stories constitutes a Bible. Moreover, there are many different types of oral Bible with different stories that can be readily adapted to meet the latest need of oral learners. Stories are amended so that they do not offend the culture of oral learners. Naming a collection of stories an 'oral Bible' implies that it has the authority of God's Word.

Advice on crafting Bible stories

Story Runners has provided what it calls a 'storytelling tip sheet' for crafting a story. Bible-crafters are told to avoid words and phrases used in some Bible translations but which are not used in everyday speech and can be confusing. Instead of sin, consider using the phrase 'disobedience to God'. Other difficult words to avoid include *righteous, forgive, atonement, baptism, sinner, repent,* and *saved.* Crafters are told they must never add facts to Bible stories. 'However, we know that a story in Luke may omit facts from the same story found in Matthew. Feel free to do the same thing to make the story shorter and understandable but don't change the meaning of the story.'[21] A crafted story is, we are told, 'based on the Scriptures, but includes background information and stylistic changes that make it interesting and appealing to various audiences.'[22]

A Bible storying consultant, J O Terry, who was a missionary to the Philippines with the Southern Baptist Convention International Mission Board for over 30 years, publishes the Bible Storying Newsletter and the *Journal of Bible Storying.* As one of the designers of the Bible storying method, Terry gives this advice: 'Before you alter a story in any way, study it carefully so that you know it well, then pray for wisdom and anointing to prepare it for your listeners to preserve the intent and accuracy of thought from God's Word and follow the Spirit's leading. Test your stories with listeners, even test the verbatim versus the oralized accounts if in doubt.'[23] One of his newsletters provides information on Rosary gospel stories. 'The basic Rosary stories of the four sets of Mysteries are being developed into a Bible Storying set of lessons or meditations for use with those where using the rosary in meditation is part of their religious worldview. The focus is on Christ and his ministry rather [than] on the Virgin Mary.'[24]

To summarise—according to the orality movement the reasons for crafting Bible stories are to make them understandable, culturally appropriate, worldview sensitive, interesting and appealing, and to avoid words that may confuse oral learners, like *sinner* and *repent*.

Here is the first part of a crafted Bible story, entitled 'Disobedience' from Exodus 20, developed by Story Runners:

> 'The Israelites camped at the foot of the mountain. God brought Moses up the mountain where he told him a lot of things. God gave Moses laws about sacrifices, and how people are to get along, and he gave him a lot of other laws too. One of the most important things God said was this: He said, "I am the One True God, I am the one who freed you from slavery and led you out of Egypt, only worship and serve me and nothing else." And he also said: "Set aside one day a week for rest, just like I did when I created the earth; remember, don't do any work." So Moses went back down the mountain and took the time to tell the Israelites all that God had told him. And they were excited, and they all said together, "We'll do everything that God said." So the next morning Moses set up an altar and sacrificed a young bull to God, allowing the blood to flow out onto the altar, and he took some of the blood and sprinkled it onto the people, and he said: "This blood is a reminder that God promises to watch over Israel and Israel promises to obey God." After that Moses went back up the mountain to be with God where he stayed forty days.'[25]

What is significant is that this story does not mention the Ten Commandments that God gave to Israel. The crafted story has simply omitted most of the commandments, effectively denying oral learners knowledge of God's moral law.

A crafted story from Luke 15.8-10 is entitled 'Lost'. A woman celebrates with her family and friends 'because she has found her lost coin. In the same way God and all his angels rejoice when *one person changes their disobedient lifestyle.*'[26] The actual words of Christ are: 'Likewise, I say to you, there is joy in the presence of the angels of God *over one sinner who repents*' (Luke 15.10). Note that the words 'sinner' and 'repent' are not used in the crafted story. And what does it mean to change a disobedient lifestyle? This story indicates the way a crafted story can pervert the Word of God.

God's Word or crafted stories?

Making Disciples asserts that 'those who have grown up in highly literate societies tend to think of literacy as the norm, and oral communication as a deviation. That is not so… Oral communication is the basic function on which writing and literacy is based.'[27] The claim, as we have already heard, is that oral learners find it difficult to follow literate-styled presentations, even if they are made orally. Indeed, 'literate stylistic features' may even confuse oral learners.[28] Obviously Scripture (God's written Word) has 'literate stylistic features', which *Making Disciples* claim can confuse oral learners. The implication is that reading the Scriptures to those who are illiterate is a waste of time, for they cannot follow 'literate-styled presentations'. But this means, in effect, that illiterate people are being denied the Word of God recorded in Scripture, as they are fed instead a diet of crafted stories by the storytellers of the orality movement.

At this point *Making Disciples* is aware that their promotion of crafted stories could be criticised as downgrading the Bible. They do not want their storytelling technique to be seen as setting oral and literate approaches in opposition to one another. 'There are examples throughout the Scriptures where both the written word of God and the spoken word of God are given prominence, often side by side. Deut. 31-33, for example, has Moses writing down the words of the Law. God instructed him to write the words down in a song. But then he also instructed him to teach the song to the Israelites so that they would always have it in their hearts and on their lips, and always remember it. Similarly in today's world, we envision a systemic approach to evangelism, discipleship, church planting and leadership development that can involve oral, audio, audio-visual media, and print.'[29]

This argument suggests equivalence between reading Scripture and learning songs. *Making Disciples* is attempting to defuse criticism of their orality method by saying that the printed Bible has a place alongside storytelling, pictures and songs. Yet the reality is that the orality movement, with its oral Bible, is in practice downgrading the role of Scripture in the eyes of four billion oral learners.

The downgrading of the written word comes from the pride of men who think that they can improve on God's Word. But the wisdom of the orality movement is foolishness in the eyes of God, for in his wisdom God has provided a written record of his revelation to mankind. God himself speaks his Word directly to us in Scripture, hence the biblical concept of God's Word. The Lord Jesus frequently quoted Scripture and referred to it as 'the Word of God' (Mark 7.9-13). When he was tempted by Satan in the wilderness he responded three times with the words, 'it is written'. Three times our Lord quoted *texts* from the *book* of Deuteronomy that had been *written* by Moses. On the walk to Emmaus with two disciples, the risen Christ, beginning at Moses and all the prophets 'expounded unto them in all the Scripture the things concerning himself' (Luke 24.27).

So we see that our Lord took a literate approach to Scripture, and often quoted the words of Scripture. Indeed, it is recorded in Scripture that he used the phrase 'it is written' or words to that effect, over thirty times during his earthly ministry. The Gospel of John was written 'that you might believe that Jesus is the Christ, the Son of God; and that believing you might have life through his name' (John 20.31). In the book of Revelation the risen, glorified Christ commanded the apostle John to 'write in a book' what he saw, and to send what he had written to the seven churches in Asia (Revelation 1.11). Clearly, Christ wanted the churches to read his words written in Scripture, and a blessing is pronounced on all who *read* and hear (that is hear it read and not 'oralised') the words of this book (Revelation 1.3).

The prophet Jeremiah draws attention to those who claim to be teaching the message of God by using their own words. But they are false prophets who speak a vision of their own hearts, and not the

Word of God. The Lord warned: 'I have not spoken to them, yet they prophesied. But if they had stood in My counsel, and had caused My people to hear My words, then they would have turned them from their evil way and from the evil of their doings' (Jeremiah 23.21-22). The command of God is clear: 'And he that has My word, *let him speak My word faithfully...* is not My word like a fire? says the Lord, and like a hammer that breaks the rock in pieces?' (Jeremiah 23.28-29). God's written Word is understandable by men, women and children and able to turn them from their sin. God speaks to the heart of man through his written Word.

In Luke 4 we have an example of the Lord Jesus teaching in the synagogue. He stood up to read, and the *book* of the prophet Isaiah was brought to him. 'And when Jesus had opened the book, he found the place where it is written' (Luke 4.17). He read from Isaiah 61.1-2, and then he closed the book and said, 'This day is this Scripture fulfilled in your ears' (v21). Notice the emphasis on literate means—the word 'book' is mentioned three times. Here is the biblical model for teaching the Gospel. We are to read and teach Scripture, the Word of God. God speaks to the heart of man through his written Word. Hence the Bible's command that pastors 'give attention to [public] reading, to exhortation, to doctrine' (I Timothy 4.13). The original Greek word 'reading' always means public, vocal reading. Therefore those who cannot read need to have the Scriptures read to them, and most illiterate believers will do all they can to learn to read the Bible for themselves.

Improving the impact of the message

Making Disciples says that after developing a basic understanding of orality, literate missionaries and ministers need to learn effective oral communication styles which are culturally relevant, for 'using cultur-ally appropriate oral forms *improves the impact* of the message'[30] (my italics). But this is contrary to Scripture. The apostle Paul determined to preach the Gospel not with 'persuasive words of human wisdom but in demonstration of the Spirit and of power' (1 Corinthians 2.4). Paul realised the futility of using persuasive words to convince an unbeliev-ing world (1 Corinthians 1.18) which regarded the message of the Cross as foolishness. He determined to preach Christ crucified *not* with the excellence of speech, *not* with culturally sensitive language, *not* with crafted Bible stories, because he understood that spiritual truth is spiritually discerned (1 Corinthians 2.14).

An inoffensive Gospel

Making Disciples points out that in many parts of the world there is open hostility to evangelistic activity. 'Crusades, mass evangelism, and public preaching are not welcome. Bible studies and open witnessing draw negative responses. In these situations storying can be more fully appreciated. Storying is not confrontational. It is not preaching. It is not overt teaching. It is merely conveying the stories of God's Word, dialoguing about them and leaving the results to God! Most of the time the hearers do not even realize that their values are changing until they can no longer deny the truth. His Word says that it will not return void or empty.'[31] Notice the assertion that crafted oral stories are 'His Word', thereby claiming that crafted oral stories have all the authority of God.

The orality movement aims to present a 'gospel' that is neither confrontational nor offensive to oral learners. The reason there is no offence is because the crafted stories do not confront sin and challenge the heart of oral learners. Crafted stories are 'not sharper than any two-edged sword, piercing even to the division of soul and spirit' (Hebrews 4.12), for they are not the Word of God but the futile, culturally sensitive words of men.

The true Gospel of Christ is not a 'conversation' or a 'story'; it is a proclamation of God's truth that is an offence to an unbelieving world because it faithfully and lovingly confronts sin and wickedness. The Lord Jesus said, 'and this is the condemnation, that light is come into the world, and men loved darkness rather than light, because their deeds were evil. For everyone practising evil hates the light and does not come to the light, lest his deeds should be exposed' (John 3.19-20). The Lord said that the world 'hates Me because I testify of it that its works are evil' (John 7.7). The Cross of Christ is an offence to those who are perishing in their sin and unbelief.

Church planting

According to *Making Disciples*, storytelling is not only appropriate to initial evangelism, it is also viable for a sustained, indigenous-led church-planting movement. The following story purports to demonstrate the power of storytelling as a church-planting initiative among oral learners in India. A Christian outreach team met a man in an Indian village who had never been to school. 'They presented the gospel using oral methods, including stories, visual aids, dramas, songs, dances, and testimonies and the man trusted Christ. He then shared his testimony with his family, who also believed and were baptized. He then went to other relatives and shared his new faith with them, using many of the same oral methods. They also believed and were baptized. He then formed a team of believers, all oral communicators, who went to neighbouring villages using the same combination of stories, dramas, songs, etc. People in those villages accepted Christ, too. Those new believers formed their own teams and they went to yet other villages, still using the same basic strategies that had been introduced in the beginning.'[32]

The remarkable claim is that unbelievers can be converted and baptized into the Christian faith and churches planted, without any knowledge of God's written Word. There is a real danger that storytelling is producing false churches, made up of people who have not genuinely repented of their sin and have not received Christ as Saviour and Lord.

Secondary oral learners

Making Disciples raises the issue of those who *prefer* to learn by oral methods although they can read. These people are known as 'secondary oral learners', a term coined by Walter Ong, father of the modern orality movement, whose teaching is dealt with in the next chapter. (The term 'preferenced oral learner' is also used to describe this group of people.) Missions-minded Christians are called to explore ways to be more effective in communicating with secondary oral learners.[33] We are told that over half of the US adult population will never read another book after high school. We are told that 'most people in the world, even most of the literate people in the world in fact, do not get much of their ideas about the world from reading. They get them from watching television, going to the movies, listening to the radio, and other forms of audio-visual communication.'[34]

A number of examples are quoted as indications of 'a growing global emergence of secondary orality, or post-literacy as some call it... The implications of this have ramifications not only on what we do in evangelism, discipleship, leader training and church planting, but also on how we do it! *We must make adjustments in the way we communicate the message of the gospel*, acknowledging that our goal, responsibility, and desire are to communicate truth in the most effective ways possible'[35] (my italics). Rick Durst, Professor of Theology at Golden Gate Seminary in San Francisco, says that to be a 'storyteller' is no longer a euphemism for someone with a loose grip on truth. 'The storyteller is becoming again the person of wisdom who knows the "good telling stories" that make and maintain community and meaning.'[36]

Making Disciples describes an experiment in new ways to communicate with secondary oral learners that is being carried out by Campus Crusade for Christ. Four types of stories are being used in the experiment. First are God's stories, which are narratives from Scripture. Second are stories of the discipler's own experience with God. Third are stories from other people's lives and video clips from movies and TV programmes. Fourth are stories from the Bible that help the new disciple develop his or her own stories that can be used to minister to others.

Making Disciples says that similar models are being launched with executives and professionals, as well as with new Christians in Sunday school classes. 'We possess knowledge of the greatest story ever told. We increasingly understand how to communicate that knowledge better with the two-thirds of the population of earth who will receive it best through storying and other oral means. In recent years we have begun to see that storying can greatly increase effectiveness *even with literate people*, including college students and business and professional people (my italics).'[37]

So we see that even among those who can read and have the Bible in their own language, but do not feel like reading, the orality movement is committed to promoting storytelling, rather than encouraging such people to read God's Word. In the eyes of the orality movement there seems to be little place for the expository preaching of God's Word.

Making Disciples concludes that because of the insights gleaned from research and collaboration, 'Christians have the opportunity to reach in our generation the billions of unreached people in the world headed to a Christless eternity. Following the example of Jesus' own witness through parables and proverbs, we can communicate the Gospel orally in a way that these unreached people can understand, respond to and reproduce. Let us therefore go forth embracing oral communicators as partners—together making disciples of all peoples to the glory of God!'[38]

There is now such confidence in the effectiveness of oral methods that organisations such as the International Mission Board (IMB) of the Southern Baptist Convention are heavily engaged in this approach. Hundreds of field teams are using storying as a primary strategy in dozens of countries. Radio ministries are becoming increasingly involved in supporting oral approaches. FEBA Radio has partnered with other agencies in Central Asia, the Middle East and North Africa in broadcasting stories. Trans-World Radio (TWR) has recently identified orality as one of five top strategic initiatives.[39]

The unbiblical nature of orality

The idea that Christians should avoid literate means in communicating the Gospel to two-thirds of the world's population is fundamentally unbiblical. Scripture is the voice of God speaking to mankind. We learn to know God through Scripture. The God of Scripture commands his people to *read* his words recorded in the Scriptures, for they testify of Christ (John 5.37). Moses *wrote* about Christ, and our Lord commenting on this said, 'But if ye believe not his *writings*, how shall ye believe my words?' (John 5.47).

The orality movement makes a tragic nonsense of the heroic labours and sufferings of past generations of missionaries who gave up all and risked their lives to take the Gospel to the uttermost parts of the world. Their great mission was to give indigenous people the Word of God in their own language. To this end they toiled, reducing many languages to a written script for the first time, thereby enriching and purifying cultures with the soul-saving doctrines of the Bible.

The flawed wisdom of the orality movement is gleaned not from Scripture but from the minds of men. From its roots in new evangelicalism and the Lausanne Movement, storytelling the Gospel represents in theory and practice a sustained attack on Scripture and the Gospel of truth. Hence the warning of the book of Jude: 'It was needful for me to write unto you, and exhort you that ye should earnestly contend for the faith which was once delivered unto the saints' (Jude 3). In the next chapter we shall learn that the theory of orality is based on the work of a Jesuit priest. We shall also learn of the link between storytelling and the emerging church.

(Endnotes)

1 *Lausanne World Plus*, 'What Do You Think, Mr. Guttenberg? The Challenges Print Evangelism Ministries Face in Meeting the Needs of Oral Cultures', by Avery Willis and James Greenelsh, October 2006

2 Cape Town 2010 website, Video, Quote from 'Communicating to Oral Learners - Introduction and Transitions', http://conversation.lausanne.org/en/conversations/detail/11520

3 Lausanne Global Conversation, 'That All May Hear', Author: Grant Lovejoy, Date: 03.06.2010, Category: Orality

4 Ibid.

5 Ibid.

6 International Orality Network website, History of ION, http://www.oralbible.com/about/history

7 Storytelling the Gospel - The Way Forward, By Jim Bowman and SD Ponraj 4-15-08, article online, http://74.53.198.191/~siutrain/images/pdfs/Perspectives.pdf

8 Lausanne Occasional Paper No. 30, 'Globalization and the Gospel: Rethinking Mission in the Contemporary World', produced by the Issue Group on this topic at the 2004 Forum for World Evangelization hosted by the Lausanne Committee for World Evangelization in Pattaya, Thailand, September 29 to October 5, 2004

9 *Making Disciples of Oral Learners*, Lausanne Committee for World Evangelization and International Orality Network, 2005, pp3-4

10 Ibid. p4

11 Ibid. p6

12 Ibid. p7

13 Storytelling the Gospel - The Way Forward, (ref 7 above)

14 *Making Disciples of Oral Learners*, p74 (ref 9 above)

15 Storytelling the Gospel-The Way Forward, (ref 7 above)

16 *Making Disciples*, p75 (ref 9 above)

17 Ibid. p124

18 Website of StoryRunners, a ministry of Campus Crusade for Christ, The Story Bible, www.storyrunners.com/story-bible

19 *Making Disciples of Oral Learners*, p117 (ref 9 above)

20 Ibid. p12

21 Storytelling Tip Sheet, http://www.storyrunners.com/documents/storytelling-tips.pdf

22 'Storytelling: some frequently asked questions' by Karl Franklin, in *Momentum Magazine*, Jan/Feb 2008, p19

23 'Oralizing Stories for Telling', by J.O.Terry, Bible Storying Consultant & Trainer http://www.churchstarting.net/biblestorying/oralizing.htm

24 The Bible Storying Newsletter, 'God's Word Story by Story to Empower Every Person Oral or Literate for Witness and Discipling Their Own', July, 2010, Vol 17 No 3, p4

25 Story Runner website, Story Set, 'Disobedience', http://www.storyrunners.com/resources/sample-story-set

26 Ibid. 'Lost', http://www.storyrunners.com/resources/sample-story-set

27 *Making Disciples of Oral Learners*, p6 (ref 9 above)

28 Ibid. p6

29 Ibid. p13

30 Ibid. p25

31 Ibid. p17

32 Ibid. pp44-45

33 Ibid. pp57-58

34 Ibid. p59

35 Ibid. p60

36 Tony Jones, Postmodern Youth Ministry, Zondervan, 2001, p27 (quoted from *Making Disciples* p61)

37 *Making Disciples of Oral Learners*, p62 (ref 9 above)

38 Ibid. p72

39 Ibid. pp67-68

Chapter 7

· Downgrading the written Word

We have seen that the Lausanne Movement for world evangelization, which was founded on the ideas of new evangelicalism, played a significant role in developing and promoting the concept of storytelling the Gospel to oral learners. Such is Lausanne's enthusiasm for oral methods that its booklet, *Making Disciples of Oral Learners,* has been translated into a number of languages. As part of its campaign to spread storytelling across the world, in 2005 Lausanne helped to establish the International Orality Network.

International Orality Network (ION)

The International Orality Network, which subscribes to the Lausanne Covenant drafted by John Stott in 1974, is a loose association of hundreds of ministries, both Western and non-Western, whose sole purpose is to spread the concept of storytelling to mission organisations and churches around the world. Its main objective is to promote training resources that include various ways and methods of implementing orality programmes.

Director of the ION, Rev Avery Willis, was of the view that past methods of evangelism, which used literature and the written word, have been a failure among people living in oral cultures. He said: 'The fact that literate, print-oriented missionaries from the West have missed this oral storying method for so long may be one of the single most serious tactical mistakes we have made in the last two hundred years. I grieve over all the time, energy and funding that I have personally directed toward print evangelism mission endeavours that missed the mark for oral learners.'[1]

The ION's promotional video, called 'Knock, Knock', explains why we need to change our approach to evangelism:

> 'The saving message of Jesus Christ is being proclaimed to more people than at any time in history. But what if there is a *barrier* that prevents countless millions, yes billions of those people, from actually hearing the message? What if 60% of the world population can't, won't or don't hear the Gospel when we share it, simply because it's coming to them through *literate means* they don't understand or relate to? They just can't hear it. There are four billion people in our world known as oral learners—an overwhelming two-thirds of the world's population. They're found in every culture group in the world. It's as if they're deaf to the Gospel, unable to hear the urgent knock on the door; unable to hear the good news because it comes to them through *literate means* that do not speak to their heart. This global reality represents an unparalleled challenge for the Gospel, a challenge that will require the church and mission organisations the world over to *radically rethink everything we're doing*. It will demand that we change our fundamental approach to evangelism, discipleship, leadership training and church planting. It will demand that we find a way to address the unique needs of these oral learners in a way they can understand, a way they can hear, really hear.'[2]

This promotional video makes two significant points. The first is that the written word is a barrier that prevents people from hearing and understanding the Gospel. The second point is that the orality movement is targeting not only illiterate people, but also those it has chosen to label as 'preferenced oral learners'. At a stroke it has extended the need for storytelling to include three billion 'oral preferenced learners'—people who in the eyes of the orality movement prefer to hear stories rather than read God's Word.

The Network now has over a hundred mission organisations and denominations in partnership. Membership organisations include: The Lausanne Movement, Youth with a Mission (YWAM), Wycliffe Global Alliance (formerly Wycliffe Bible Translators, name changed in 2011), Trans-World Radio (TWR), T4 Global, Story Runners, Summer Institute of Linguistics (SIL), The Seed Company, Scriptures In Use, One Story Partnership, The International Missions Board of the Southern Baptist Convention (IMB), Heart Sounds, Global Recordings Network, The God's Story Project, Faith Comes By Hearing, E3 Partners, Call2All, and Campus Crusade for Christ.

A key goal of the ION is that by 2020 mission agencies in the West, and the rest of the world, will be aware of the need to communicate by means of oral methods. The hope is that a majority of mission organisations will prepare their missionaries to use oral strategies in evangelism, discipleship and leadership training. The ION would like to see at least thirty percent of seminaries and Bible schools worldwide offering courses in oral strategies.[3]

Orality Breakouts

The booklet, *Orality Breakouts: Using Heart Language to Transform Hearts*, was prepared for the Cape Town Congress. While *Making Disciples of Oral Learners* emphasised evangelism, discipleship and church-planting, *Orality Breakouts* focuses on oral communication styles to transform lives. In the foreword, Avery Willis welcomed his readers to the world of orality: 'This book is about how God is breaking down resistant fields of mission endeavour, how God is bringing alive His stories to unreached people groups, and how God is birthing His Church around the world. Join in and witness what God is doing with orality.'[4]

Douglas Birdsall, Executive Chair of the Lausanne Committee for World Evangelization, is enthusiastic in his praise of *Orality Breakouts*: 'We are engaging one of the great new frontiers of Mission… Our friends in the International Orality Network have rediscovered a teaching method from Jesus that works in this millennium—storytelling the Bible to oral *preference* learners. This book provides case studies, methods, and resources for every leader and every lay person to become an effective storyteller of the Bible.'[5]

Paul Eshleman, Vice-President of Campus Crusade for Christ, is equally enthusiastic: 'The world is being captured by the use and power of storytelling. Every church, organization, and mission must equip itself to reach and disciple the millions who *prefer* to learn orally. The first-hand accounts in this book will give you a vivid look at this breakthrough strategy.'[6] Jerry Wiles of Living Water International comments: 'This is a great book that I believe can be a momentum builder for the Orality Movement. My hope and prayer is that it has wide distribution and gets into the hands of key leaders worldwide who are serious about the Great Commission. Some comments we are hearing from those participating in orality training workshops are, "transformational, historic, a new and better way of making disciples".'[7]

From the above discussion it is clear that the orality movement is sweeping through the evangelical world at an alarming rate. Again we must note that the focus is now on so-called 'preferenced oral learners'. This means that storytelling is now being promoted in churches where the congregation can read. How has this remarkable transformation come about? To fully understand the orality phenomenon we need to recognise that the underlying motivation comes from two directions. First is the work of a Jesuit priest, Professor Walter Ong, and second is the influence of the emerging church.

Walter Ong – father of the orality movement

According to *Making Disciples*, 'it is essential that literate church leaders seek to understand orality'.[8] And to help church leaders learn about oral communication they are referred to the research and thinking of Professor Walter Ong, regarded by many as the father of the orality movement. Indeed, Ong's book, *Orality and Literacy* (1982), is referred to by *Making Disciples* as a respected academic work that offers a lengthy, technical discussion on the nature of orality and the impact that writing has had on oral communication.[9] The aim of Ong's book is to draw out the contrasts between orality and writing.[10] But we are not told that the author of *Orality and Literacy* is a Jesuit priest.

Primacy of oral cultures

The underlying premise of Ong's analysis is that human beings in so-called 'primary oral cultures', untouched by writing in any form, possess and practise great wisdom.[11] He says that writing 'is a particularly pre-emptive and imperialist activity that tends to assimilate other things to itself even without the aid of etymologies'[12] (etymology is the study of the history of words). He claims that 'oral cultures indeed

95

produce powerful and beautiful verbal performances of high artistic and human worth, which are no longer even possible once writing has taken possession of the psyche.'[13] He explains that oral cultures 'use stories of human action to store, organize, and communicate much of what they know. Most, if not all, oral cultures generate quite substantial narratives or series of narratives.'[14] He argues that 'oral art forms which developed during the tens of thousand of years before writing obviously had no connection with writing at all'.[15] He insists that the spoken word is primary, 'and yet from the start it was destined – or in another way, doomed – to be supplemented with all the devices and even gadgetry which have reduced it more and more to space'.[16]

Problems of the written word

Ong's theory is based on the idea that in many situations oral communication is superior to the written word. In *The Presence of the Word*, he argues that for certain uses of language, literacy is not only irrelevant but is a positive hindrance.[17] He maintains that we are so grounded in a literate ideology that we think writing comes naturally. 'We have to remind ourselves from time to time that writing is completely and irremediably artificial.'[18] He repeatedly refers to orality as natural and to writing as artificial. His basic sympathies are clear, for he alludes to written text as 'dead' and to speech as more 'real'.[19]

Ong describes a number of problems with what he calls the 'technology of writing'. He claims that writing 'cannot be directly questioned or contested as oral speech can be because written discourse has been detached from its author'.[20] He asserts that 'one of the most startling paradoxes inherent in writing is its close association with death. This association is suggested in Plato's charge that writing is inhuman, thing-like, and that it destroys memory.'[21] He argues that 'the condition of words in a text is quite different from their condition in spoken discourse... written words are isolated from the fuller context in which spoken words come into being. The word in its natural oral habitat is a part of a real, existential present. Spoken utterance is addressed by a real, living person to another real, living person.'[22] The problem with writing is that 'words are alone in a text... in writing something, the one producing the written utterance is also alone. Writing is a solipsistic operation.'[23] (Solipsism is the philosophical idea that only one's own mind is sure to exist; it holds that knowledge of anything outside one's own mind is unsure.[24])

The theories of Walter Ong form the foundation of the orality movement. The premise of his work is that human beings need to return to their earlier, evolutionary, primitive heritage of myth, fable, story, image, symbol and icon. The written word is degraded, while the spoken word and visual image are eulogised as being more closely connected to human consciousness. He draws attention to the fact that some societies 'have regarded writing as dangerous to the unwary reader, demanding a guru-like figure to mediate between the reader and the text. Literacy can be restricted to special groups such as the clergy.'[25] Here we should note that in past centuries the Roman Catholic Church restricted the reading of the Bible to the priest.

Professor Daniel Chandler, an expert in the structure and meaning of language, comments on Ong's approach: 'In such a framework, to the Jesuit Father Ong, writing surely represents the Fall of Man from Edenic existence. He declares explicitly that: "All reductions of the spoken word to non-auditory media, however necessary they may be, attenuate and debase it, as Plato so intensely felt".'[26] Chandler says that Ong propagates the idea that the written word is problematic, for it weakens and degrades the spoken word.

The fallacy of Ong

Ong's orality theory has two flaws. The first is his evolutionary approach that presents a false view of primitive man living with the spoken word alone, which he claims is the ideal method of communication. Ong sees the advent of writing as a Fall from a utopian, primitive world in which myth, fable, story, image, symbol and icon were the methods of communication. His claim that cultures in which there is no written word possess and practise great wisdom is disingenuous, for the stark reality is that most oral cultures are ruled by superstition and ignorance. There is no doubt that cultures without the written word are at a grave disadvantage, for they have no way of accurately recording their history, no way of recording scientific discoveries and no books with which to educate their population. Perhaps we should not be surprised that a Jesuit priest appears to find great virtue in primitive cultures ruled by ignorance and superstition.

But the Bible teaches us that man did not evolve, but was created by God and endowed with the gift of language, the ability to reason, and, no doubt, with the innate ability to write. The first chapters of Genesis, which explain the creation of heaven and earth, the making of the woman from the rib of Adam, the marriage of Adam and Eve, and the temptation and Fall in the Garden of Eden, come from the written records of Adam, preserved in the godly line of believers and collected and recorded in Scripture by Moses.

The second flaw in Ong's theory is that he has drawn a false dichotomy between the oral and the written word. He has sought to show that oral communication and written communication stand in opposition to one another. And the outcome of this invalid comparison is that the 'natural' oral word is superior to the 'artificial' written word. But Ong is wrong, for the spoken word and the written word are not in competition but are complementary to each other. Scripture is clear on this point, for God has revealed himself through both the spoken and the written word.

On Mount Sinai God *spoke* all the words of the Ten Commandments to Israel, and then the finger of God *wrote* the commandments on tablets of stone as a permanent record for all people for all time. And God commanded his prophet Moses to write his words, 'and Moses wrote all the words of the Lord' (Exodus 24.4). And Moses took the Book of the Covenant, which he had written, and read it in the audience of the people, and God instructed Moses to teach the commandments (Exodus 24.7, 12). God's people are commanded to 'keep his commandments and his statutes which are written in this book of the law' (Deuteronomy 30.10). When the men, women and children of Israel appeared before the Lord in the feast of tabernacles, the priests were commanded to 'read this law before all Israel in their hearing' (Deuteronomy 31.12). When the Israelites entered the Promised Land, Joshua built an altar and wrote upon the stones a copy of the Law of Moses and 'he read all the words of the law, the blessings and cursing, according to all that is written in the book of the law. There was not a word of all that Moses commanded, which Joshua read not before all the congregation of Israel' (Joshua 8.34-35).

God's character and moral laws are revealed in his written Word, the Scriptures, which are for all people for all time. The Word of the Lord endures forever (1 Peter 1.25). The apostle Peter teaches that Christians, who have been born again through the Word of God, are to desire the pure milk of the Word in order to grow in their spiritual life (1 Peter 1.23-2.2). We must read and study God's written Word, the Scriptures, which are given by the inspiration of God (2 Timothy 3.16). Christians are commanded to preach and teach sound doctrine which comes from a diligent study and correct interpretation of God's written Word. The Gospel of Jesus Christ has been made manifest and by the prophetic Scriptures made known to all nations, according to the commandment of the everlasting God (Romans 16.25-26). Clearly, God's written Word is indeed for all people and for all nations and for all times. What is more, God's *written* Word guards his people against error and heresy that come from false teaching. The Church of Rome has preserved its sway over so many people by keeping them from God's written Word.

The Jesuit Order

Here we need to remember that the author of *Orality and Literacy* was a Jesuit priest, for there can be no doubt that Ong's research and writings were shaped by his Jesuit training. As a priest, Ong had been active in ministry since his ordination in 1946 (he entered the Society of Jesus in 1935). For decades he celebrated daily Mass, and weekly he administered the sacrament of Reconciliation. He regularly directed others in the Spiritual Exercises of Saint Ignatius of Loyola, the founder of the Jesuit Order.

It is important to understand that the Jesuit Order, given papal authority in 1540, was committed to the restoration of the authority of the Roman Catholic Church by ruthlessly destroying the Protestant Reformation. With their vow of total obedience to the Pope and their strict military-style training, the Jesuits became feared across Europe as the 'storm-troopers' of the Catholic Church.[27] They correctly perceived that the strength of the hated Reformation lay in making the Scriptures available to the ordinary man in the street. They realised that the Protestant doctrine, that the Word of God is the sole basis of spiritual truth and sufficient for all matters of doctrine and conduct, fatally undermined the dogmas and traditions of Rome. And so a fierce antagonism has always existed between Bible-believing Christianity and Roman Catholicism.

William Tyndale, who translated the New Testament into English in 1525, was singled out as an archheretic by Rome. He was convinced that the way to God was through his Word, and that Scripture should be available even to the common people. The reformed historian John Foxe describes an argument with a 'learned' but 'blasphemous' clergyman, who had asserted to Tyndale: 'We had better be without God's laws than the Pope's.' With deep passion, Tyndale made his historic response: 'I defy the Pope, and all his laws; and if God spares my life, I will cause the boy that drives the plough in England to know more of the Scriptures than the Pope himself!'[28] Tyndale had come to the conclusion (true in all ages including our own), that it is impossible to establish the people in Christian truth, except the Scriptures be plainly laid before their eyes in their mother tongue.

William Whitaker, a prominent sixteenth-century theologian and Master of St. John's College, Cambridge, believed that the Roman Catholic Church had intentionally deprived many people from gaining access to Scripture and therefore the Gospel. In his book, *A Disputation on Holy Scripture: Against the Papists, Especially Bellarmine and Stapleton* (1588), he wrote: 'Who does not see that the Scriptures are taken from the people, in order that they may be kept in darkness and ignorance, and that so provision may be made for the safety of the Roman Church and the papal sovereignty which could never hold its ground if the people were permitted to read the Scriptures.'[29]

The Jesuits were distinguished by their hatred for the Protestant Bible. In the eyes of the Jesuits, to permit lay people to read the Scriptures was a detestable crime that had to be eradicated at all costs to preserve papal authority. Their strategy was to challenge, pervert and where possible destroy the Word of God. Opposition to the Bible, even before the Jesuits, resulted in the martyring of Tyndale and the public burning of the New Testament to keep it from the people. The Bible was even put on the Roman Catholic Index of Forbidden Books. Many godly men and women, because of their work in making the Scriptures available to ordinary people, perished in the flames of the

Roman Catholic Inquisition, which reached its height in the sixteenth-century to counter the Reformation. Although the Bible was removed from the Index of Forbidden Books in 1966, this was for reasons of expediency only, and did not mean a genuine change in opposition to the teachings of the Bible. The atrocities of the Jesuits are a matter of historical record. They stopped at nothing – torture, assassination, the stake, political intrigue and more – in their determination to destroy the Reformation and the light of God's redeeming grace that comes from knowledge of the Bible.

Covert attack on Scripture

Ong's ideas expressed in *Orality and Literacy* undoubtedly have the support of the Roman Catholic Church. As a faithful and obedient Jesuit priest, he harboured a deep antagonism towards the written Word of God. The inevitable consequence of Ong's theory is that the written Word of God should be replaced by the oral word of the storyteller. And so the age-long war against Scripture waged by the Roman Catholic Church now seeks to achieve its purposes, with the help of Lausanne, through the orality movement. Today we do well to remember the ongoing enmity against Scripture manifested by the Church of Rome.

The doctrinal compromise of Lausanne is demonstrated by the way it has latched onto the work of a Jesuit priest in an attempt to confer academic respectability on storytelling in place of biblical teaching. In the mind of the orality movement the great commission is to be ac-complished by 'a movement of cross-cultural Bible story experts who have the skill to train people to engage unreached oral learners with a complete set of Bible stories in the local language that are tailored to transform their unique worldview.'[30]

In its zeal for the orality movement, *Making Disciples* 'challenges churches and other Christian organizations to ride the next wave of Kingdom advancement by developing and implementing methods for effective oral strategies. Partners, networks, seminaries, mission agencies, conference and workshop leaders, as well as other Christian influencers are called upon to recognize the issues of orality in the world around them. We all need to become intentional in making disciples of oral learners. We need to raise awareness, initiate oral communication projects and train missionaries and local leaders in chronological Bible storying as an effective church-planting strategy.'[31]

Storytelling and the emerging church

Storytelling is a key technique of the emerging church movement. Brian McLaren, elder spokesman of the emerging church, has made several observations about storytelling. In an interview he said: 'I would be honored to be characterized as a storyteller – and as a story-hearer as well, trying to discern the stories implicit in messages, news, and other information... The Bible itself is a collection of stories, and in some cases, it's a collection of duelling stories, stories competing for the privilege of framing a community's actions in the present and hopes for the future.'[32] He argues that the best preachers believe in the story's magic. 'The challenge for those communicating in the emerging culture is to use the wonderful benefits of storytelling to tell The Story to a culture that is looking for a context.'[33]

In his book, *The Story We Find Ourselves In* (2003), McLaren presents Christianity as a 'story'. He contrasts this new way of thinking with the traditional way of defining Christianity by a set of doctrinal beliefs. He uses an idealised postmodern storyteller called Neo, to draw a contrast between the new narrative form of Christianity and the traditional doctrines which are shown to be outdated and no longer relevant. McLaren claims the narrative version of Christianity is more effective in reaching seekers who are put off by doctrine. He develops a framework of storytelling that is anti-doctrine, which he claims is the only acceptable framework for the postmodern world. He describes characters who complain that Christianity is 'a bunch of doctrines', or a 'set of beliefs'. Doctrine is thus the enemy to be overcome by McLaren's new version of emerging Christianity.

In *Experiential Storytelling: (Re)Discovering Narrative to Communicate God's Message* (2003), 'emergent' author Mark Miller says storytelling is the best way for the Church to reach today's postmodern generation. He writes: 'What if we removed all of the argumentative language, replaced it with beautiful narratives, and let people feel the power of story? Instead of trying to convince people to accept a list of spiritual laws, how about placing individuals in the story, allowing them

DOWNGRADING THE WRITTEN WORD

to learn and interact with God's character? What if we told our story in a holistic manner engaging all of the God-given senses?'[34]

He explains why stories have the power (especially with the post-modern generation) to touch a person at all levels, for they connect with people and cause them to think. He writes: 'When a story becomes personal and people begin to become unsettled and challenged by it, then they have been touched in a place where facts fear to tread. It is a place so personal that it can spark an inner transformation.'[35] He addresses the traditional sermon and wants pastors to consider narrative preaching.

In line with the thinking of the emerging church the International Orality Network promotes the idea that 'all the arts – storytelling, singing, dancing, drama, drawing, sculpture, and more – are interrelated ways to tell The Story, especially to oral learners.'[36] To this end the International Orality Network has set up the Music and Arts Task Force which 'aims to foster a global movement that will use all the arts in culturally appropriate ways in order to make disciples... We promote the arts as important means of expressive communication among oral learners. The task force encourages and equips people who want to use the arts in their ministries by building their vision, by providing practical training, and by linking them with effective resources and tools.'[37]

Lausanne Commitment 2011

The Cape Town Congress ended by expressing its total commitment to the orality agenda. The following actions have been agreed by the Lausanne Commitment of 2011.

'As we recognize and take action on issues of orality, let us:

1. Make greater use of oral methodologies in discipling programmes, even among literate believers.

2. Make available an oral format Story Bible in the heart languages of unreached and unengaged people groups as a matter of priority.

3. Encourage mission agencies to develop oral strategies, including: the recording and distribution of oral Bible stories for evangelism, discipling and leadership training, along with appropriate orality training for pioneer evangelists and church-planters; these could use fruitful oral and visual communication methods for communicating the whole biblical story of salvation, including storytelling, dances, arts, poetry, chants and dramas.

4. Encourage local churches in the Global South to engage with unreached people groups in their area through oral methods that are specific to their worldview.

5. Encourage seminaries to provide curricula that will train pastors and missionaries in oral methodologies.'[38]

Real agenda of the orality movement

The real agenda of the orality movement, which is based on the flawed theories of a Jesuit priest and the weird practices of the emerging church, is to downgrade Scripture in the eyes of two-thirds of the world's population. The actions of the orality movement represent a serious and sustained attack on God's Word. Having asserted that the written word is a barrier to the Gospel, the orality movement is committed to creating an oral Story Bible as a matter of priority. In this way it is replacing the divine wisdom of Scripture with the trivial messages of the storyteller, and the trivial images of the emerging church. Visual images, chants, art, dance, poetry and drama are actively promoted as effective methods for teaching the truths of the Christian faith, as we saw in chapter 5. The result is a distorted, non-biblical version of Christianity that is based on stories—a counterfeit version of Christianity that is without a doctrinal base, that feeds its adherents on crafted stories.

Lausanne's campaign to promote the storytelling movement comes from its unquestioning acceptance of the flawed academic work of a Jesuit priest. The age-long war against the Bible has found a powerful ally in the Lausanne Movement. The tragedy is that many true Christians, especially in the Third World, are being deceived and misled by the persuasive promotion of the orality agenda.

The Word of God has been recorded by the Holy Spirit in Scripture. Today, we hear the voice of God through his written Word. Christian believers are commanded to preach the Word in season and out of season (2 Timothy 4.2), for it is 'the Holy Scriptures, which are able to make you wise for salvation through faith which is in Christ Jesus. All Scripture is given by inspiration of God and is profitable for doctrine, for reproof, for correction, for instruction in righteousness, that the man of God may be complete, thoroughly equipped for every good work ' (2 Timothy 3.15-16).

(Endnotes)

1 *Lausanne World Plus*, 'What Do You Think, Mr. Guttenberg? The Challenges Print Evangelism Ministries Face in Meeting the Needs of Oral Cultures' by Avery Willis and James Greenelsh, October 2006

2 The International Orality Network, Orality issues, Communication – 'Knock, knock' promotional video, http://www.youtube.com/watch?v=PQItsLKapkM

3 The Mission Exchange, *Excelerate*, Issue 1, 2009, 'Gazing on God's Glory and Telling His Story', pp12-13

4 *Orality Breakouts*, on-line version, published by International Orality Network, 2010, Foreword, p7 http://www.heartstories.info/sites/default/files/Foreword.pdf

5 Ibid. Testimonials, S. Douglas Birdsall, Executive Chair, Lausanne Committee for World Evangelization

6 Ibid. Testimonials, Paul Eshleman Vice-President, Campus Crusade for Christ, International - Director, Finishing the Task, USA

7 Ibid. Testimonials, Jerry Wiles, President, Living Water International, USA

8 *Making Disciples of Oral Learners*, Lausanne Committee for World Evangelization and International Orality Network, 2005, p24

9 Ibid. p21

10 Walter Ong, *Orality and Literacy – The Technologizing of the Word*, Routledge, first published 1982, reprinted 2000, p5

11 Ibid. p9

12 Ibid. p12

13 Ibid. p14

14 Ibid. p140

15 Ibid. p10

16 Walter Ong, (1967): *The Presence of the Word: Some Prolegomena for Cultural and Religious History*. New York: Simon & Schuster, pp 320-1, reference cited from 'Biases of the Ear and Eye' by Daniel Chandler, phonocentric, last modified: 10/11/2011 http://users.aber.ac.uk/dgc/Documents/litoral/litoral2.html

17 Ibid. p21

18 Walter Ong, ([1978] 1983): 'Literacy and Orality in Our Times' in Winifred B Horner (Ed.): 'Composition and Literature: Bridging the Gap'. Chicago: University of Chicago Press, p 129, cited from 'Biases of the Ear and Eye' by Daniel Chandler, http://users.aber.ac.uk/dgc/Documents/litoral/litoral2.html

19 *Orality and Literacy*, p81 and p101 (Ref 10 above)

20 Ibid. p78

21 Ibid. p81

22 Ibid. p101

23 Ibid. p101

24 Wikipedia, Definition of solipsism

25 *Orality and Literacy*, p93 (Ref 10 above)

26 Walter Ong, (1967): *The Presence of the Word*, p322, (Ref 16 above)

27 Website of Bible Questions Answered by GotQuestions.org, Question: "Who are the Jesuits, and what do they believe?"

28 Nation Master Encyclopaedia, William Tyndale, http://www.nationmaster.com/encyclopedia/William-Tyndale#_ref-1

29 William Whitaker, *A Disputation on Holy Scripture against the Papists especially Bellarmine and Stapleton* (Morgan, Penn.: Soli Deo Gloria Publications, nd. [1588; 1849], p210. Cited from the article 'Biblical Authority and the King James Bible' by John D Woodbridge

30 *Lausanne World Plus*, 'What Do You Think, Mr. Guttenberg? The Challenges Print Evangelism Ministries Face in Meeting the Needs of Oral Cultures', by Avery Willis and James Greenelsh, October 2006

31 *Making Disciples of Oral Learners*, p79 (Ref 8 above)

32 Patrolmag website, 'Saving Stories: An Interview with Brian McLaren', by Kenneth Sheppard On November 24, 2010

33 Cited from the Worship Leaders Manual, written By Mark Tittley, p64, website, www. scribd.com/doc/21794305/Worship-Leader-Manual

34 Mark Miller, *Experiential Storytelling : (Re)discovering Narrative to Communicate God's message*, 2003, Zondervan, p29

35 Ibid. p41

36 International Orality Network website, Task Forces, Music and Arts, http://www.oralbible.com/what-you-can-do/volunteer

37 Ibid.

38 The Lausanne Movement, The Cape Town Commitment: A Confession of Faith and a Call to Action (2011), paragraph 2 D, Discerning the will of Christ for world evangelization, Oral cultures http://www.lausanne.org/ctcommitment

Chapter 8

Ecumenical Alpha

Rev Nicky Gumbel was one of the main speakers at the Cape Town Congress in 2010. His talk, 'How to do Evangelism in the 21st Century', provided an opportunity to promote the popular Alpha Course, which he directs from Holy Trinity Brompton (HTB), an Anglican church situated in central London. Alpha is widely acclaimed as an evangelistic tool, and since its inception in 1991 has spread rapidly across the world; it is even popular in the USA, with *Christianity Today* referring to Alpha as the 'the fastest-growing adult education program in the country'. In 1998, *Alpha News* made it clear that the course is a means of drawing together both Protestants and Catholics, for 'Alpha bids to focus on common ground'.[1] Alpha's approach fitted perfectly with Lausanne's ecumenial vision for the Church.

Alpha endorsed by leading evangelicals

Alpha has been enthusiastically endorsed by leading evangelicals. Rick Warren, Senior Pastor of Saddleback Church in the USA, says: 'It's great to see how Alpha has been used to reach people with the good news of Jesus Christ, who wouldn't normally come to church. Alpha is one of the most effective evangelism tools for the 21st century... and is very complementary to helping seekers connect with The Purpose Driven Life.'[2] Bill Hybels, Senior Pastor of Willow Creek Community Church in the USA, says: 'Alpha is one of the best known evangelistic programs in the world. I don't think anybody rejoices more in its effectiveness than I do... We applaud the vision and work of Alpha to connect the unconnected to the life of the local church and to relationship with Jesus Christ.'[3]

Wayne Grudem, Professor of Biblical and Systematic Theology, Trinity International University, Illinois, says: 'I highly recommend the Alpha course to everyone interested in discovering how the Christian faith can be exciting and life-changing in the modern world. The course is biblically sound, understandable, and practical. It will have a significant impact on people's lives and it will strengthen every church in which it is held.'[4]

Alpha's charismatic background

The term 'Alpha' is an acronym built on the following ideas: A for Anyone interested in the Christian faith; L for Learning and Laughter, for it is possible to learn about the Christian faith and have fun at the same time; P for Pasta and Pie, for eating a meal together gives people an opportunity to get to know each other; H for Helping one another, for the small group provides a chance to discuss issues raised in the talks; A for Ask Anything, for Alpha is a place where no question is regarded as too simple or too hostile.

Underpinning the Alpha course is a very strong charismatic influence. The home of Alpha, Holy Trinity Brompton, was visited by charismatic 'prophet' John Wimber, founder of the Association of Vineyard Churches, a number of times during the 1980s and 1990s. A seminal event occurred in May 1994, when Nicky Gumbel attended a meeting of church leaders to hear Eleanor Mumford, assistant pastor of the South-West London Vineyard Church, described her recent visit to the 'Holy Spirit revival' taking place at Toronto Airport Vineyard Church in Canada, soon to be known as the 'Toronto Blessing'. She explained her remarkable experiences of the power of God, and then she prayed for those in the meeting to be filled with the Holy Spirit.

Here we need a word on the Toronto Blessing. This bizarre phenomenon, which originated from the Toronto Airport Vineyard Church in 1994, swept through the charismatic world with great speed. Sometimes called the 'laughing revival', it captured headlines in both the Christian and secular media of the time. Its most notorious features were helpless, involuntary laughter from individuals and whole congregations, even when the content of an address was serious. In addition, extraordinary and uncontrolled bodily movements and the production of animal noises, such as lion-like roars, were common. Another feature was the large numbers of people falling backward and lying motionless for hours on end, sometimes quietly, sometimes laughing or crying, and afterwards claiming that they had received the Holy Spirit as they lay on the floor. The many visitors to Toronto seemed able to 'catch the blessing' and physically take it home to their own churches, where the 'laughing revival' would break out.

The Toronto Blessing phenomenon was hugely controversial, even dividing opinion among charismatic churches. Needless to say, the whole thing was profoundly unbiblical and probably involved some form of suggestibility or altered states of consciousness, induced by 'stage hypnosis'. It lasted only a short time and led to no true revival, despite all the claims, testimonies and publicity that accompanied it.

With this background, it is not difficult to see that Eleanor Mumford's prayer had a remarkable affect on everyone present, including Nicky Gumbel, who suddenly realised that he was late for a staff meeting, and so rushed back to HTB. After apologising for being late, he spoke briefly about the account of the Toronto 'revival' he had just heard. He then concluded the staff meeting with prayer, asking the Holy Spirit to fill everyone in the room. The church newspaper, *HTB in Focus* (12 June 1994), provides a record of this dramatic event: 'The effect was instantaneous. People fell to the ground again and again. There were remarkable scenes as the Holy Spirit touched all those present in ways few had ever experienced or seen. Staff members walking past the room were also affected. Two hours later some of those present went to tell others in different offices and prayed with them where they found them. They too were powerfully affected by the Holy Spirit – many falling to the ground. Prayer was still continuing after 5 pm.'[5]

In one of his Alpha talks (video 3, talk 9), Gumbel speaks about the Toronto Blessing. He explains how Eleanor Mumford 'told us a little bit of what she had seen in Toronto… it was obvious that Ellie was just dying to pray for all of us… then she said, "Now we'll invite the Holy Spirit to come", and the moment she said that one of the people there was thrown, literally, across the room and was lying on the floor, just howling and laughing… I experienced the power of the Spirit in a way I hadn't experienced for years, like massive electricity going through my body… One of the guys was prophesying. He was just lying there prophesying.'[6]

With the influence of the Toronto Blessing in the background, it is no surprise that three Alpha sessions have a charismatic bias, dealing with the filling of the Spirit, speaking in tongues and healing through prayer. To understand the Alpha course we must recognise that it is thoroughly charismatic in content and theology.

Nicky Gumbel addresses the Cape Town Congress

Nicky Gumbel started his talk to the Cape Town Congress by affirming that his testimony is summed up in a verse which he loves. He then quoted Romans 1.16 from the Jerusalem Bible of the Roman Catholic Church, 'For I am not ashamed of the gospel, because it is the power of God for the salvation of everyone who has faith.'[7] Gumbel told the Congress that 15 million people in 169 countries had done the Alpha course, from right across all the different parts of the Church and all the different denominations. He said he had the privilege in the last few years of meeting and hearing the stories of some of these people: 'And when I hear their testimonies about the power of God to change lives I am always so moved.'

Gumbel said that the Gospel is both words and actions. 'We are not just concerned about the conversion of individuals, as important as that is, but we are concerned about the transformation of our society.' He concluded, 'This is an exciting time to be a Christian and my appeal is that we as Christians, we as the Church of Jesus Christ entrusted with the gospel of Jesus Christ, should stop fighting one another and unite together to take this message to the world.'[8]

Alpha's ecumenical heart

Central to Gumbel's message is the plea that Protestants and Catholics should stop fighting each other and unite to take the Gospel to the world. In Alpha talk 14 he makes the following statement: 'One of the exciting things that is happening in these days is that God is lowering the denominational barriers and people don't mind so much anymore whether you are a Methodist or a Baptist, whether you are a Roman Catholic or an Anglican. These are not the significant things.'[9] The implication of this short statement is that doctrinal differences between the Roman Catholic Church and Protestant denominations are no longer significant. With this amazing claim the Alpha course effectively sweeps aside the Reformation.

In February 2004, after shaking hands with the Pope in the Vatican, Gumbel said, 'It was a great honour to be presented to Pope John Paul II, who has done so much to promote evangelization around the world... what unites us is infinitely greater than what divides us.'[10] Those who attend the Alpha course are taught that the differences between Protestants and Catholics are 'totally insignificant compared to the things that unite us... we need to unite around the death of Jesus, the resurrection of Jesus; the absolute essential things at the core of the Christian faith on which we are all agreed. We need to give people liberty to disagree on the things which are secondary.'[11] Gumbel's call for unity between Protestants and Catholics lies at the very centre of the Alpha message.

Alpha in a Catholic context

The Alpha course in a Catholic context is run in thousands of Catholic parishes around the world, hosted either by the parish priest or a lay member of the parish. Preacher to the Papal Household, Father Raniero Cantalamessa, has endorsed the course. 'In my opinion Alpha accomplishes an incredible task, in making people interested in faith and in making faith relevant to the modern man. I especially appreciate the ecumenical spirit of the Alpha course: There is no pressure on anybody to join a different denomination, but just to join Jesus and to put Jesus at the centre.'[12]

A lay Catholic explains how Alpha strengthened his faith. 'I was brought up a Catholic, but all my life I attended church out of obligation, out of duty. I was asked along to Alpha at St George's parish, Norwich... On one of the evenings I was prayed for, and I received the Holy Spirit. I had a smile from one ear to the other. My church life has now intensified greatly. I go to a weekly prayer meeting at St George's and I am a children's liturgy catechist. I also do catechism with the parents of children who are being baptised. I am now reading at Mass, and participating in many more of the parish activities.'[13]

The Alpha course has a number of talks to help Catholics have a better understanding of their faith. These talks are used after the standard Alpha sessions have been completed. A UK edition of *Alpha News* carried an advert, entitled 'Catholic Follow-Up', which provided information on the extra videos that deal with subjects such as 'Mary and the Saints', 'Roman Baptism' and 'Getting more out of the Mass'. Seven talks are given by the preacher to the Papal Household, Raniero Cantalamessa.[14]

Catholicism 201 is a follow up course to Alpha specially developed for Catholics by Father James Mallon, a priest of Saint Benedict Parish in Halifax, Nova Scotia. Father James is an adviser to Alpha for Catholics in the USA and Canada. He has been running the Alpha Course in his various parishes since 2001, and later that year he created the Catholic 201 programme, which covers such topics as 'The Church', 'Sacraments and Sacraments of Initiation', 'The Sacrament of Healing' and 'The Eucharist'.[15] Catholicism 201 has now been run in more than 20 countries and is being translated into Spanish.[16] Clearly the Catholic Church sees nothing in the Alpha course that is a danger to them or is contrary to the doctrines of Rome. Indeed, Alpha is proving to be very popular among Catholics, apparently helping them to have a better understanding of their faith.

Church of Rome endorses the Alpha Course

In May 2005, President of the Pontifical Council for Promoting Christian Unity, Cardinal Walter Kasper, addressed the Alpha Conference in Stuttgart, Germany, with these words: 'Alpha courses, which came originally from an Anglican background, are also opportunities to strengthen ecumenical togetherness among Christians and a joint proclamation of faith in Christ in today's world.'[17]

In June 2010 the week-long Alpha International Conference (Europe, Middle East and Africa) was attended by more than 1200 delegates, including more than 20 Catholic archbishops, bishops and their representatives from across the world. Cardinal Archbishop Vincent Nichols of Westminster saluted the work of Alpha: 'This evening I have heard wonderful testimonies about the work of Alpha in prisons, in poor countries, in many, many different circumstances. I pray that God will guide us all in this journey of deeper and deeper understanding and greater visible unity between our churches.'[18]

In his address to the Conference Nicky Gumbel explained why Christian unity is so vital. He said that the Lord Jesus wants unity now.

'He wants the Church to be united – completely, visibly united. Of course, we hope that one day that will take place. But in the meantime, I think sometimes God gives us a glimpse of what visible unity would look like. I think this event is an example of what visible unity looks like. As we look around this church today, we see a foretaste of visible unity.'[19]

Head of Alpha in the Catholic Church, Kitty Kay-Shuttleworth, summed up the Conference: 'It has been a wonderful week as Christians from many different denominations have come together with a shared love of Christ and vision for evangelization.'[20]

Another gospel

Despite the widespread acceptance of Alpha by evangelical Christians and Roman Catholics, many true believers are highly critical of Alpha. Pastor Chris Hand, of Crich Baptist Church, in Derbyshire, in a critique of Alpha, entitled *Falling Short* (1998), says that 'Subjects such as God as Creator, the majesty and glory of his being, his holiness, his wrath against sin, and the judgement that is to come are either completely absent or else hugely understated. Sin is underplayed in its gravity and the whole approach is man-centred.'[21] Alpha misrepresents the nature of God's forgiveness 'by toning down the significance of sin and the need for full repentance'.[22]

The Holy Spirit Weekend Away is the high point of the Alpha course. The aim is that participants should be filled with the Holy Spirit and learn to speak in tongues. One participant explains, 'Nicky talked about the gifts and tongues, and at the end of his talk, he asked the Holy Spirit to come. I was just totally overcome… The tears started running and everything was happening to me—it was just a wonderful experience, and something I truly never expected.'[23] Pastor Chris Hand offers a word of caution. He says that 'many of these experiences are not genuine but are induced through an "altered state of consciousness"… It is not the Holy Spirit who is introduced to people on the Weekend Away. Having failed to encounter Christ in their mechanical "praying of a prayer", they then fail again to encounter Him on the Weekend Away.'[24]

A host of problems arise from the failure of Alpha to present a biblical portrait of the character of God or to give a true description of the fallen human condition. 'It fails to offer a meaningful gospel but has simply set forth a loving God whom we are invited to believe in without any proper explanation of what He is like or what He requires of man… The very success claimed for Alpha as a great evangelistic tool proves in the end to be hollow.'[25] Alpha's criteria of what constitutes a Christian are very broad. 'As long as we have the Spirit of God we are all brothers and sisters… We can hold opposing and contradictory views about the message of salvation but we are "brothers and sisters" if we have had the experience of the "Spirit". This is a disastrous view to hold.'[26]

Pastor Chris Hand concludes that while Alpha believes in reaching the lost, it tells them a different Gospel. 'It is full of love but has no place for telling sinners the truth. There is a belief in the Holy Spirit but no room found for the evidences of his working in true repentance and faith. It is a substitute for the real thing… The time has come to call it for what it is—it is another God, another Jesus, and another gospel. It is not building the true church but is constructing a false one which has no appetite but only scorn for biblical truth. For evangelicals, it is no friend of ours and we should avoid it at all costs.'[27]

Michael Penfold, in his article, 'The Gospel According to Gumbel', says that it is small wonder that after a weak explanation of sin and wrath, and a confused presentation of the Cross, Gumbel's invitation to accept Christ comes up short. 'Once anyone prays the prayer to receive Christ, they are assured by Gumbel, "If you've asked Him to come in, He has." This "all you have to do is ask" mentality has lulled millions into a false sense of security.' Penfold concludes with this warning: 'Alpha is neither solemn enough, nor sound enough, nor safe enough to be used by any individual or church who takes biblical evangelism seriously. May God grant faithful Christians to take a stand against this erroneous course.'[28]

The Alpha Agenda

Nicky Gumbel's method of teaching the Gospel fits perfectly with the Lausanne campaign for world evangelization. But there are two major problems with the Alpha course. First, it presents a flawed, compromised view of the Gospel of truth. It fails to describe the holy character of the God of Scripture, it fails to describe the sinfulness of sin, and it fails to call sinners to true repentance that leads to salvation

(2 Corinthians 7.10) through faith in the finished work of Christ on the Cross. The danger is that nominal Alpha Christians who have not truly repented of their sin, who have not truly turned to Christ in saving faith and been soundly converted, are being added to church congregations. Those who would preach Christ and him crucified should avoid Alpha like the plague.

Second, Alpha is deeply ecumenical in approach, claiming that there are only minor differences between evangelical Christianity and the Church of Rome. Nicky Gumbel's constant cry is that Christians should stop fighting each other and unite. The booklet, *The Alpha Course – Friend or Foe?*, emphasises the ecumenical nature of the course: 'It is difficult to imagine for one moment that the main purpose of Alpha is to present the Gospel of Jesus Christ. Yes, there is profession that this is so, there is training to do so. But, the overall impression coming from Alpha internationally is that *unity* through the ecumenical movement is the purpose of Alpha. *Unity*, with the Vatican in control is the ultimate purpose of Alpha.'[29] This message makes the Alpha course acceptable to the Lausanne cause, for the real agenda of both appears to be to unite 'Christians' under the authority of the papal Father. We can safely conclude that Alpha, like the Lausanne Movement, is not a tool in the hand of God, but a tool in the hand of the ecumenical movement.

(Endnotes)

1 *Alpha News*, March-June 1998, cited from, 'The Alpha Course – Friend or Foe?' by WB Howard, Editor of Despatch Magazine. Information gathered from the Alpha Conference in Brisbane, Australia, 1998, p7

2 Alpha website, What people say, Church leaders, http://uk.alpha.org/leaders

3 Ibid.

4 Alpha website, Academia, http://www.alpha.org/academia

5 Cited from, A History of the Revival of 1992-1995, Holy Trinity Brompton, Richard M Riss, www.grmi.org/Richard_Riss/history/htb.html

6 The Alpha Course by Carol Brooks, cited from website, In Plain Site, Section 10A, The Contemporary Church, 'Christian' Courses Alpha, http://www.inplainsite.org/html/the_alpha_course.html,

7 Cape Town 2010 website, Nicky Gumbel, Integrity - How to Do Evangelism in the 21st Century, Videos, http://conversation.lausanne.org/en/conversations/detail/10984

8 *International Alpha News*, No. 52, Dec 2010 - Mar 2011, 'What Nicky said...' p3

9 Cited from Elizabeth McDonald and Dusty Peterson, *Alpha – the unofficial guide*, St

Matthew Publishing, Second revised edition 2003, p170

10 *Alpha News*, March-June 2004, p7

11 Cited from Cephas Ministry Newsletter, The Alpha Course – is it the final answer or a fatal attraction? newsletters.cephasministry.com/alpha_fatal_attraction.html

12 Alpha website, Other Leaders & Church Leadership, http://www.alpha.org/media-room/leaders

13 Alpha website, Philip Hook, Norfolk, Alpha in a Catholic context, http://uk.alpha.org/type/alpha-catholic-context

14 Cited from *Alpha – the unofficial guide*, p125 (Ref 9 above)

15 Alpha Friends website, http://www.alphafriends.org/catholics/after-alpha

16 Catholicism 201 website, http://www.catholicism201.ca/index.php?option=com_content&view=category&layout=blog&id=77&Itemid=465

17 Christ Life website, Catholic Leaders Encourage the Alpha Course, www.christlife.org/sharefaith/EndorseAlpha.html,

18 *Alpha News International*, No. 51, Vincent Nichols, Sep – Dec 2010, p3, http://issuu.com/alpha-international/docs/ani_51

19 *Alpha News International*, No. 52, Why does unity matter so much to Jesus? December 2010 – March 2011, http://issuu.com/leilabagnallalpha/docs/international_alpha_news_dec10_-_mar_11

20 *Catholic Herald* website, 'Bishops applaud Alpha', by Staff Reporter on Friday, 2 July 2010

21 Chris Hand, *Falling short*, Day One, 1998, p64

22 Ibid. p74

23 *Alpha News*, April 1994, p9, cited from *Falling Short* p77

24 *Falling short*, p90

25 Ibid. p90

26 Ibid. p95

27 Ibid. p98

28 Webtruth website, 'The Gospel According to Gumbel (the Alpha Course)', Michael J. Penfold, http://www.webtruth.org/articles/what-is-the-gospel-21/the-gospel-according-to-gumbel-(the-alpha-course)-40.html

29 'The Alpha Course – Friend or Foe?' by WB Howard, editor of Despatch Magazine, information gathered from the Alpha Conference in Brisbane, Australia, 1998, p7

Chapter 9

Lausanne's love for the poor

The Lausanne Movement lays claim to special Christian love for the world's poor and suffering. The Lausanne Committment, *A Confession of Faith and a Call to Action* (2011), declares: 'Such love for the poor demands that we not only love mercy and deeds of compassion, but also that we do justice through exposing and opposing all that oppresses and exploits the poor. We must not be afraid to denounce evil and injustice wherever they exist.'[1]

An advance paper for the Cape Town Congress, entitled 'Poverty and Wealth', was written by Corina Villacorta of World Vision International and the Rev Harold Segura, a Baptist evangelical pastor. The paper was presented by Villacorta in the session, 'Wealth, Poverty and Power'. (Both authors are working to bring the Catholic and Evangelical Protestant churches in Latin America closer together.[2])

The authors contend that 'while the accumulation of wealth by individuals and large corporations is unprecedented in modern times, the magnitude of poverty and inequality that millions of people experience today continues to be unacceptable and appalling'. They assert that 'a renewed and revitalized understanding of the meaning of Christian social responsibility is crucial'. They stress that 'we have a moral imperative to pursue justice in the world, to engage in the struggle against poverty, to join our voices in a denunciation of immoral wealth and to defend human rights and dignity'. They insist that 'we urgently need to consider the overwhelming reality of structural sins brought on by the startling inequity present in our world today. The stark reality of wealth and the stark reality of poverty mutually explain each other. One cannot be understood apart from the other... Poverty cannot be understood in isolation without reference to the immoral levels of wealth in the world.'[3]

The advance paper told the Congress that Third World poverty 'calls us to assume our prophetic role if we understand that one of the fundamental causes of poverty is injustice. Almost a century after the Declaration of Human Rights, an incredible step taken by the states of many nations, we witness the violation of the dignity of the poor on a day-to-day basis as they experience the violation of fundamental rights. The unequal distribution of resources and accumulated wealth is one of the most blatant ways in which injustice manifests itself. The existence of unprecedented levels of concentration and accumulation of wealth by individuals, corporations and nations; all indicate that something is fundamentally wrong with the way humankind has organized the economy, power relationships and society as a whole.'[4]

The authors expressed concern that 'the economic interests behind production systems are imperilling life as we know it on the planet today, depleting natural resources at an alarming rate. The main parties responsible for the emission of pollutants are industries that possess infrastructures worth billions of dollars. These infrastructures will need to be transformed, and/or dismantled in order to create environmentally friendly means of production of goods and services. Unless key actors are willing to give up resources, wealth and power, there is no way to turn back and rescue the earth's sustainability.'[5]

So in the name of 'saving the environment' the authors appear to be calling for the infrastructure of the world's industrial nations to be dismantled. One can only wonder how it is that a Christian Congress has engaged itself in such blatant political rhetoric. The underlying assumption of this paper is that poverty is caused by social injustice and the structural sins perpetrated by rich Christians in the West. The assertion that 'the stark reality of wealth and the stark reality of poverty mutually explain each other', is consistent with socialist ideology that entirely ignores the link between wealth and the biblical work ethic. The political message of this paper is similar to that found in Ronald Sider's *Rich Christians in an Age of Hunger* and accords with John Stott's socialist agenda.

Poverty and Micah Challenge

Joel Edwards, the international director of Micah Challenge and former head of the UK's Evangelical Alliance, wrote an advance paper for the Congress entitled, 'Promise and the Gospel of Well-being'. The aim of Micah Challenge, a global coalition of the World Evangelical Alliance (WEA) and the Micah Network, is to halve world poverty by 2015. The Micah Network brings together 330 Christian organisations providing relief, development and justice ministries throughout the world. The WEA claims to embrace 420 million evangelical Christians in 127 countries worldwide.

In his paper Edwards claims that at the dawn of the new Millennium a political miracle took place. 'For the first time a meeting of world leaders took place in New York for what was described as an "unprecedented gathering" convened by the United Nations. The United Millennium Summit gave birth to a dream in which nations promised to slash extreme poverty by half by the year 2015. These promises contained eight wide but measurable goals by which the preventable indignity endured by over a billion people would be brought to an end.' This covenant, which came to be known as the Millennium Development Goals (MDGs) has, according to Edwards, amounted to 'more than fiscal promises to the poor. This was an historic and moral contract to "spare no effort... freeing the entire human race from want".'[6]

The MDG goals include eradicating extreme poverty and hunger; achieving universal primary education; promoting gender equality; empowering women; ensuring environmental sustainability; and establishing a global partnership for development.

Micah Challenge, a global coalition of Christians, sees its role as holding governments to account. 'We are establishing a global movement to encourage deeper Christian commitment to the poor, and to speak out to leaders to act with justice.' Edwards asserts that our task 'is to strip away the negotiated excuses and rediscover a gospel of well-being which is totally consistent with the mission of God in the world and which cares and speaks up for the poor without muzzling our faith in Christ.'[7]

Micah Challenge is so utopian in its ideas that it believes world poverty and social injustice can be eradicated through political action guided by the United Nations. It has great faith in the promises of world leaders to slash extreme poverty. Yet its optimism is misplaced, for it takes no account of the sinful nature of man that causes corruption, sloth, deceit and greed—sins that all too often lead to poverty.

The hole in World Vision's gospel

Richard Stearns, one of the keynote speakers at the Cape Town Congress, expressed his frustration with Christians in the USA in his book, *The Hole in Our Gospel* (2009). Stearns is the chief executive of World Vision, a Christian humanitarian organisation that has endorsed the Universal Declaration of Human Rights and the United Nations Convention on the Rights of the Child. It is a major aid distributor for the UN World Food Programme.

Stearn's basic premise is that the real Gospel entails a public and transforming relationship with the world, resulting in a social revolution to help the poor, compassion for the sick, and liberation for those who are victims of political, social or economic injustice. He believes that the 'hole' in the Gospel is collective neglect of the poor and the marginalised, because Christians in the USA have reduced the good news of Jesus Christ to a 'personal transaction with God, with little power to change anything outside our own hearts'.[8]

A critique by Pastor Paul Van Noy, founder of Candlelight Christian Fellowship in the USA, describes *The Hole in Our Gospel* as 'the newest danger to come against true believers in the Church Age. It promotes a false gospel within a socialistic philosophy. It fails miserably in its hermeneutic, is ecumenical in focus, promotes human performance as a method of pleasing God, and believes people on earth can do good to "usher in the Kingdom".'[9]

A review on Amazon makes the point: 'In his enthusiasm to convince the West to address social injustices, Stearns forgot that Jesus came to the world to call people to repentance and obedience. That is the whole Gospel, which is sadly and glaringly missing in Stearn's Gospel.' Another critic comments: 'Stearns sounds more like an Emergent calling on Christians to embrace the social gospel than he does one who affirms the salvific nature of the cross and resurrection that then moves us to action.'[10] And here is perhaps the most perceptive comment: '*The Hole in our Gospel* is largely theological liberalism. If you are not current on liberalism it's often defined thus: A God without wrath, brought men without sin into a kingdom without judgment, by ministrations of Christ without a cross. It's an easy thing to buy into without realizing that all the important parts are completely left out, and you now have a new shell gospel that nobody really objects to, but does not capture the essence of the original.'[11]

Stearns gave a presentation to the Cape Town Congress that was consistent with the views expressed in his book. He said the American Church has a weak and one dimensional Gospel that defends the status quo, makes no demands on their wealth, and lacks the power to change the world. He said the radical Gospel of Jesus Christ was intended to launch a social and spiritual revolution on earth, but sadly the Church over the generations has failed to be good news. He also claimed that over the generations Christians in the USA have been so compromised that they systematically exterminated the native American people groups. His call is for the Church to actively engage in social activities to improve the lives of the poor in the developing world.[12]

Stearns said he sometimes dreamt of what could happen if Christians responded to his call and gave lots of money to the poor. In his dream the year is 2025 and the Secretary General of the United Nations announces that the Millennium Goals to reduce world poverty have been achieved, signalling good news for the world's poor. The reason for this amazing success is that Christians in the Global North have given more than $250 billion a year to alleviate world poverty. In announcing this great achievement the Secretary General notes that not since the end of the Second World War has the world come together with such a spirit of the common good in pursuit of such a noble cause. Could Lausanne 2010 be a turning point for the world? Stearns thinks that if Christians in the West embrace the whole Gospel and not the gospel with a hole in it then his dream could come true. The massive redistribution of resources from the Global North to the Global South could start with the four thousand leaders at the Cape Town Congress, who have it within their power to change the world for Christ.[13]

Stearns seems to believe the Church of Jesus Christ and the United Nations should work together as partners to alleviate world poverty. Yet the United Nations is an organisation denominated by the spirit of the age, steeped in secular humanism and committed to a multi-faith agenda. Scripture commands Christians to be separate from the world, for what fellowship is there between light and darkness, between Christ and Belial? (2 Corinthians 6.14-18). So the large hole is in Stearns social gospel, which is based on the false notion that Christ came into the world to organise a social revolution.

New International Economic Order

The Lausanne Movement asserts that the cause of Third World poverty is economic injustice. We are told that the structural sins of the West have brought on the startling inequality in wealth that is apparent in our world today. At the Cape Town Congress Rene Padilla expressed concern about the globalisation of what he calls an unjust economic system (by which he means capitalism), which he says is 'destroying humankind'. In the Lausanne paper, *An Evangelical Commitment to Simple Life-style*, we heard John Stott refuse to acquiesce in the intolerable injustice that causes one quarter of the world's population to endure grinding poverty, while another quarter enjoys unparalleled prosperity. We are told that this economic injustice can only be overcome by redistributing wealth from rich to poor. Ronald Sider has called for a redistribution of wealth to help the poor and oppressed in the Third World. Singing from the same socialist hymn sheet, Richard Stearns called for a massive redistribution of resources that he said could start with the four thousand Congress leaders gathered in Cape Town.

Lausanne is doing all it can to persuade its supporters that a New International Economic Order is the solution to global poverty. Here we should note that Lausanne's support for a new economic order is entirely consistent with the ideology of socialism. Indeed, socialist dogma strives for an economic system that will reduce inequality and eliminate want forever. According to the British Socialist Party, 'capitalism creates immense inequality and deprivation when the potential exists for providing a decent life for all.'[14] *A Socialist Manifesto* says, 'we seek a fair, non-disruptive and easily implemented, *redistribution of wealth* that will fight strenuously against both poverty and obscene wealth'.[15] Socialists believe that 'the main cause of the perseverance of poverty is rich people preventing poor people from rising up out of poverty.'[16] So the New International Economic Order advocated by Lausanne is a socialist economic system which redistributes wealth from rich to poor. The reality is that Lausanne has a political agenda to join the struggle for a new socialist world economic order.

Real cause of poverty

To understand the real causes of poverty we need to turn to Scripture. The world created by God was very good. The LORD planted a garden, eastward in Eden, provided a river to water it, and out of the ground 'made every tree grow that is pleasant to the sight and good for food' (Genesis 2.9). The LORD God put the man in the garden to work and keep it and commanded the man: 'Of every tree of the Garden you may freely eat; but of the tree of the knowledge of good and evil you shall not eat, for in the day that you eat of it you shall surely die' (Genesis 2.16-17). When Adam and Eve rebelled against God's command and wilfully ate of the forbidden tree, they faced the consequences of their rebellion. God said to Adam, 'Cursed is the ground for your sake; in *toil* you shall eat of it all the days of your life. Both *thorns and thistles* it shall bring forth for you, and you shall eat the herb of the field. In the *sweat* of your face you shall eat bread till you return to the ground' (Genesis 3.17-19). The words 'toil' and 'sweat' are used to show that man will have to work hard to produce the food he needs to survive.

A consequence of the Fall is that this world is a hostile environment, and life is uncertain and full of trouble and hardship. Another consequence is that man, because of his fallen, sinful nature, is prone to laziness. Indeed, slothfulness has always been identified as one of the traditional seven deadly sins. Scripture is forthright in identifying laziness as a cause of hunger and poverty. The Bible's wisdom literature warns that 'laziness casts one into a deep sleep, and an idle person will suffer hunger' (Proverbs 19.15). Therefore, 'do not love sleep, lest you come to poverty; open your eyes, and you will be satisfied with bread' (Proverbs 20.13).

Wisdom literature emphasises the relationship between laziness and poverty that is denied by worldly thinking. 'I went by the field of the lazy man, and by the vineyard of the man devoid of understanding; and there it was, all overgrown with thorns; its surface was covered with nettles; its stone wall was broken down. When I saw it, I considered it well; I looked on it and received instruction: A little sleep, a little slumber, a little folding of the hands to rest; so shall your poverty come like a prowler, and your need like an armed man' (Proverbs 24.30-34). And Scripture also warns of the relationship between a wayward lifestyle and poverty. 'Do not be among winebibbers or among gluttonous eaters of meat; for the drunkard and glutton will come to poverty, and drowsiness will clothe them in rags' (Proverbs 23.20-21).

Hard work and bread to eat

Hard work is the biblical answer to poverty. The man 'who tills his land will be satisfied with bread' (Proverbs 12.11). God promises that he will bless his people Israel, and make them abound in prosperity, if they obey his commandments. Blessed shall be 'the produce of your ground… blessed shall be your basket and your kneading bowl' (Deuteronomy 28.4-5). The biblical principle is that the LORD will not *normally* allow the righteous to go hungry. 'The LORD will not allow the righteous soul to famish… the righteous eats to the satisfying of his soul' (Proverbs 10.3; 13.25). Therefore David could confidently affirm: 'I have been young, and now am old, yet I have not seen the righteous forsaken nor his children begging bread' (Psalm 37.25). And the Lord Jesus himself said that our heavenly Father, who knows what things we need, would always provide for his people (Matthew 6.32-33). A believer, who is a new creature in Christ with a new nature, is motivated to diligence and productiveness out of a love for his Saviour. His old propensity towards slothfulness—and all other sins—has been replaced by a desire to live a godly life.

Yet it is wrong to think that there will be no poor Christian people. God has providential dealings with his people, and circumstances can be such that a believer does not have the opportunity or means to work. For example, a believer can be made redundant because of a downturn in the economy. And we know that a collapse of the national and international economic and financial systems can cause many to experience poverty, as during the Great Depression of the 1930s and the economic problems since 2008. Moreover, in many nations Christian believers are subject to persecution that may lead to economic hardship and great suffering. What is more, illness and disability may strike, preventing work. But while all these things occur in the providence of God, our heavenly Father knows what things we have need of.

Scripture is clear that there will always be poor in society.[17] Some are poor because of their sin and slothfulness, some because of their choice of lifestyle, some because of illness or disability, and some because of unfavourable local or international circumstances over which they have no control. However, the biblical principle is that the believer will do all he can to find work and support his family, and fulfil the biblical injunction to be able to give to those in need (Ephesians 4.28), whereas the lazy choose the way of idleness.

Helping the poor and needy

Scripture is clear that Christian believers are to help the poor and needy among them. 'If there is among you a poor man of your *brethren*, within any of the gates in your land which the LORD your God is giving you, you shall not harden your heart nor shut your hand from your poor *brother*, but you shall open your hand wide to him and willingly lend him sufficient for his need, whatever he needs' (Deuteronomy 15.7-8). The apostle John says that helping the poor is a manifestation of Christian love for the brethren: 'But whoever has this world's goods, and sees his *brother in need*, and shuts up his heart from him, how does the love of God abide in him?' (1 John 3.17). James says that if a *brother or sister* is poorly clothed and lacking in daily food, a fellow believer demonstrates his faith by giving the poor brother or sister the things which are needed for the body (James 2.15-16). The apostle Paul says that 'if anyone does not provide for his own, and especially for those of his household, he has denied the faith and is worse than an unbeliever' (1 Timothy 5.8). Christian compassion compels believers to care for the poor and needy among the brethren, and especially the needy in their own family. We have the example of Macedonian (Gentile) believers providing a generous gift to the suffering believers living in Judea (Acts 11.29-30).

But the Christian is to be generous towards the unbelieving poor as well. The biblical principle of gleaning teaches that when the farmer reaps the harvest of his land, he shall not wholly reap the corners of the field, nor shall he gather the gleanings of the harvest (Leviticus 19.9). Deuteronomy 24.19–21 stipulates that owners allow the needy, *including the foreigner*, to gather the grain that remains after the reapers have made a single sweep of their fields. The practice of gleaning was rooted in the desire to care for the poor and needy, and incorporates the principle that they should work hard for their provision. There is kindness and generosity towards the poor that enables them to preserve their dignity.

We see this biblical principle illustrated in the life of Ruth, the Moabitess. Boaz, following the law of God, allowed Ruth to glean in his field, from morning until evening, thereby enabling her to work to provide food for herself and Naomi. Following this principle, Christians of our day should do what they can to help the poor to find work that will enable them to feed their families. The apostle Paul instructs believers to do good to all people (Galatians 6.10). But there is nothing in Scripture to say that believers must redistribute their wealth to the poor of the whole world, especially as part of a political agenda.

Biblical work ethic

Scripture taken as a whole supports an economic system that respects private property and the work ethic. A biblical work ethic comes from the Christian duty to be diligent and to do everything as to the Lord and not to men, for believers serve the Lord Christ (Colossians 3.23-24). The Bible teaches that workers are to be obedient to their earthly employers in sincerity of heart, 'as to Christ; not with eye service, as men pleasers, but as bondservants of Christ, doing the will of God from the heart' (Ephesians 6.5-6). Proverbs teaches that wisdom, which comes from the fear of the Lord, is more precious than silver and gold, for 'length of days is in her [wisdom's] right hand; in her left hand riches and honour' (Proverbs 3.16). Therefore 'by humility and the fear of the Lord are riches and honour and life' (Proverbs 22.4). Proverbs 31 gives the picture of the virtuous hard-working wife. Based on these Scriptures, the Christian faith, particularly since the Reformation, has taught an ethic of hard work among believers. This biblical teaching, known as the Protestant work ethic, has undoubtedly contributed to the economic success of the West.

Yet Scripture provides the strongest possible warning that the love of money is the root of all kinds of evil. Our Lord said that we cannot serve two masters: we cannot serve both God and money (Matthew 6.24). Those who desire to be rich, who are taken over by a longing for material things, fall into temptation and a snare which greatly harms their spiritual life. The Christian is exhorted to flee materialism and to follow after righteousness, godliness, faith, love, patience and meekness (1 Timothy 6.6-11).

However, Scripture is also clear, as we have seen above, that those who are lazy are likely to remain poor. 'He who has a slack hand becomes poor, but the hand of the diligent makes rich' (Proverbs 10:4). The apostle Paul took a strong stand against those who were idle. He said, 'if anyone will not work, neither shall he eat' (2 Thessalonians 3.10). Socialism denies these two biblical truths: it denies that hard work produces wealth and it denies that laziness causes poverty.

Conclusion

The socialism of the Lausanne Movement is a profoundly unbiblical ideology. The focus on Third World poverty is designed to produce guilt among Christians in the West, persuading them that the answer is a socialist economic order that redistributes the world's resources. But the Lausanne model is a recipe for disaster that will not help the world's poor.

The major problem with socialism is that it disregards biblical teaching about fallen human nature and assumes that people act in a morally upright fashion when their basic needs are met. This is why socialistic systems tend to become dysfunctional. Winston Churchill summed it up: 'Socialism is a philosophy of failure, the creed of ignorance, and the gospel of envy. Its inherent virtue is the equal sharing of misery.'[18]

Nowhere in the book of Acts did the early church attempt to introduce a socio-economic revolution. The real commission of the Church is not to eliminate world poverty but to preach the Gospel to the lost, to those with poverty of spirit. The true mission of the Church is to bring the good news of Christ to the spiritually poor, to bind up hearts broken by the consequences of sin, to proclaim liberty to those held captive by evil, to open the prison to those enslaved by the spiritual forces of darkness. For the Gospel is the power of God unto salvation to everyone, both rich and poor, who repent of their sin and turn to Christ in faith.

(Endnotes)

1 The Lausanne Movement, The Cape Town Commitment: A Confession of Faith and a Call to Action (2011), We love God's world, paragraph 7c

2 Interview with Rev Harold Segura by John Allen Jr, National Catholic Report senior correspondent, p3 http://natcath.org/mainpage/specialdocuments/Interview_Harorld_Segura. pdf

3 Cape Town 2010 advance paper, 'Poverty And Wealth', Author: Corina Villacorta and Harold Segura, Date: 20.07.2010, Category: Poverty & Wealth

4 Ibid.

5 Ibid.

6 Cape Town 2010 advance paper, 'Promise and the Gospel of Well-being', Author: Joel Edwards, Date: 20.07.2010, Category: Poverty & Wealth

7 Ibid.

8 A review of *The Hole in our Gospel* (2010), Richard Stearns, by Ryan Dueck, http:// rynomi.wordpress.com/2010/06/08/the-hole-in-our-gospel-review/

9 A review of *The Hole in our Gospel* (2010) by Pastor Paul D. Van Noy, Candlelight Fellowship, Idaho. Cited from The Lighthouse website. http://www.lighthousetrailsresearch. com/blog/?p=5214

10 Amazon review of *The Hole in Our Gospel* by Richard Stearns. Two star review posted, May 4, 2010 by Kyle E. Mcdanell

11 Amazon review of *The Hole in Our Gospel*, One star review, Liberalism lurks here, posted February 28, 2010

12 Cape Town 2010 Congress Video, Wealth, Poverty and Power - The Hole in our Gospel, Author: Richard Stearns, Date: 24.10.2010, Category: Poverty & Wealth, http://www.lausanne. org/en/multimedia/videos/ct2010-session-videos.html

13 Ibid.

14 Socialist Party Manifesto 2010, Capitalism's limits, http://www.socialistparty.org.uk/ partydoc/Socialist_Party_manifesto_2010/4

15 A Socialist Manifesto by Eric v d Luft, Gegensatz Press, 2007, page 42

16 Ibid. p45

17 Our Lord said, 'For ye have the poor always with you' (Mt 26.11, Mk 14.7, John 12.8)

18 As quoted in The New American Newspeak Dictionary (2005) by Adrian Krieg, p. 96

Chapter 10

Lausanne's feminist agenda

The historic Lausanne Covenant of 1974, signed by multitudes of respected Christian leaders from around the world, called upon Christians to share God's 'concern for justice and reconciliation throughout human society and for the liberation of men and women from every kind of injustice'. The Manila Manifesto of 1989 affirmed 'that the gifts of the Spirit are distributed to all God's people, women and men, and that their partnership in evangelization must be welcomed for the common good'.[1] In 2004 the Lausanne Movement called 'on the Church around the world to work towards full partnership of men and women in the work of world evangelization by maximizing the gifts of all'.[2] Underlying these statements was the firm belief that women should have a leadership role in the Church.

In a presentation to the Cape Town Congress, entitled 'Integrity – Men and Women', Elke Werner, the senior associate for women in the Lausanne Movement, developed the argument for social justice for women in the Church. She stated that the Lausanne Covenant's call for the liberation of men and women from every kind of injustice had not been achieved. She said, 'As we look at the reality of this world, we have to admit that we have often times failed to voice our concern for justice for women. We have failed to liberate women from oppression. In many instances, in our own churches women are being oppressed. Women in Christian families are beaten by their husbands, and this evil is often supported by a wrong teaching on submission to one's husband. We have kept women out of positions of leadership just because they are women. We have disregarded their God-given spiritual gifts and have kept them to work in the kitchen, rather than in evangelism or teaching adults according to their spiritual gifts.' She concluded: 'God has created us men and women to work side by side—may it be so in the church, as women and men live together and serve our God in harmony, mutual submission, respect, love and peace.'[3]

An advance paper prepared for the Cape Town Congress, entitled 'The Partnership of Males and Females in the New Global Equilibrium', written by husband and wife team Leslie Anne Neal Segraves and Chad Alan Neal Segraves, identifies barriers to the equality of partnership of men and women in the Church. They say that 'women in both the West and the East have felt restrictions placed upon them, not only by the world, but also often by their Christian brothers and sisters'.[4]

The authors explain that their paper seeks 'to demonstrate the biblical and missiological worldview of those who believe God can (and does) equip both males and females with leadership and teaching gifts to be used in completing His mission.'[5] They refer to the apostle Paul to support their argument. 'The Apostle Paul instructs Timothy to "entrust (Paul's teachings) to reliable people (anthropos) who will also be qualified to teach others" (2 Tim. 2.2). Paul, a careful and brilliant writer uses the Greek word that includes both men and women, rather than the Greek word used specifically for men. Given this fact, and others learned from an in-depth study of pertinent passages, we believe that God gives leadership/teaching gifts not only to men, but also to women, and that releasing women to use leadership and teaching gifts positively impacts the Great Commission.'[6] Their assertion is that Scripture teaches that both men and women should be in leadership roles in the Church.

Real meaning of 'anthropos'

A paper by Bible researcher Michael Marlowe provides advice on the interpretation of the word 'anthropos'. He explains that the Greek word 'anthropos', especially in its plural form ('anthropoi'), is often used as a collective term (like the English 'mankind'), which obviously is meant to include both males and females; but this is not the whole story, for when 'anthropos' is used in reference to a particular individual, that individual is always male. He explains that 'anthropos' is never used in reference to an individual female: 'Whenever a particular person is introduced as an "anthropos", that person is invariably male. If the person is female, the word gyne "woman" is used instead. In this respect then, the word "anthropos" has the same range of meaning as the English word "man," which can be used in a gender-neutral inclusive sense, or as the ordinary word for "male human being," and, like "anthropos", it is never used in reference to an individual woman... Sometimes it includes both sexes, sometimes it refers specifically to males, as opposed to females. If there is any question about the sense in any given instance we must examine the context.'[7]

Clearly Bible translators across the centuries have understood the word 'anthropos' in the *context* of Paul's letter to Timothy to refer to the male sex. So 'anthropos' is translated as 'faithful *men*' in the King James Version, the New King James Version, the English Standard Version and the New American Standard Bible; as 'reliable *men*' in the NIV and as 'steadfast *men*' in Young's Literal Translation of the Bible. To use this verse to declare that the apostle Paul was advocating female leadership in the Church is clutching at straws. Michael Marlowe comments, 'The Segraves' argument is dishonest and ridiculous. Just because Paul uses anthropoi here, they conclude that this nullifies 1 Timothy 2.12. Is not the instruction in 1 Timothy 2 part of what Timothy "has heard" from Paul (2 Timothy 2.2), which he is here instructed to teach?'[8]

Argument for joint leadership in the Church

A key argument advanced in favour of joint church leadership is that of social justice. The Segraves' paper claims that the Church has been slow to address the injustice that continues for spiritually gifted women. A Western woman complains: 'Sundays are the saddest days of my life. I feel unaccepted and of little value when I walk into the church.' And a highly qualified South Asian woman tells of her suffering: 'When I come home, I am nobody! And I am silenced in my church! I would have given my life to serve the church, but I am not allowed to speak or participate in anything.'[9] Moreover, keeping the discussion of shared leadership 'in a theological ivory tower avoids the issues of injustice and identity (causing the pain to remain), does not take into account the gifting of the Holy Spirit (who gives gifts without regard to gender), and slows the task of the Great Commission (causing fewer labourers to operate in their giftedness)'.[10]

The Segraves say that husbands should be encouraged 'to share in housework and childcare so that women can also pursue and use their gifts. Both husbands and wives should encourage their spouse to use all their spiritual gifts. Both husbands and wives should care for children, and women should not be limited to their biological function.'[11] But the Segraves' advice that husbands share in housework and childcare, thereby releasing their wives to take on leadership roles in the Church, is contrary to Scripture. Indeed, the apostle Paul emphasises the home-making role of women. Younger women are admonished 'to love their husbands, to love their children, to be discreet, chaste, homemakers, good, obedient to their own husbands, that the word of God may not be blasphemed' (Titus 2.4-5).

At the Cape Town Congress, in the multiplex session, 'Men and Women: A Powerful Team for the Completion of the Great Commission', the Segraves explained their commitment to full partnership of men and women based on gifts. Chad said he had learned that he fights against the Fall when he seeks to empower his sisters in the Body of Christ to use every gift they have been given including teaching, preaching and leading. He said that it is about Jesus and multiplying his workers for his mission. His wife said as a woman she had learned that she works against the Fall when she uses every gift that God has given her, including the gift of leadership.

The message to emerge from the Congress is that women should have an equal role in preaching and leading the Church. To stress the point, Costa Rican theologian Ruth Padilla Deborst preached at a plenary session from Ephesians 2. In another presentation the Congress was told that the apostle Paul, when he encountered the Lord Jesus, became an advocate of equality and mutuality between men and women. Three important passages in Paul's letters (1 Corinthians 14; 1 Timothy 2 and Ephesians 5), that obviously teach male headship in church leadership, are summarily dismissed as being taken out of context. The conclusion is that the Church needs to make room for female leaders in the broader Body of Christ. Women must be encouraged to minister God's Word to both men and women.

One delegate was so upset by the feminist agenda that was being propagated that he made the following comment: 'I was very disappointed in the Lausanne leadership in allowing the extremely one-sided viewpoints related to men and women in Christian ministry. A prime example was the Multiplex [the 4,000 delegates were given 4-5 Multiplexes on different topics to choose from during that time] on men and women. It was totally feminist, spent most of its time preaching feminism, and ignored that there is another viewpoint on the matter. In addition to the total lack of balance and Christian charity toward other viewpoints, how they handled Scripture, twisting it to fit their viewpoints, was sad to see, and a terrible precedent to allow in the Lausanne Movement which does not bode well for its future.'[12]

Mutual submission in marriage

To continue the feminist agenda, husband and wife team, David Claydon (Senior Adviser to Lausanne) and his wife Robyn Claydon (Vice-Chair of the International Lausanne Committee) dealt with the issue of equal partnership in marriage. David Claydon stressed mutual submission in marriage by quoting Ephesians 5.21 and simply ignoring Ephesians 5.22-24, which teaches that wives must submit themselves to their own husbands. Claydon was adamant that God is the head of his household and that he and his wife practise *mutual* submission. 'When the marriage relationship is seen in terms of power lodged in one person, therefore submission required of the other, there is, of course, no equality.' He concluded: 'So we can see from biblical teaching that marriage enables us to mutually empower each other. To encourage the exercise of each other's gifts, whatever they happen to be, to value each other's strengths and to listen to each other's opinions and so to graciously forgive and share in decision making.'[13]

Robyn Claydon then stressed her absolute belief in mutual submission. She posed the question: 'What does mutual submission in marriage look like? It looks like equality, that is what it looks like. It *does* look like equality, and that's what we are trying to suggest today. There is no *but* after equal. We are not equal, *but*—we are equal in the eyes of God and we mutually submit to each other as we minister in the home, in the church and in the community.'[14] Indeed, the equality of the Claydons is such that when they preach together, as they often do, one starts the sermon and the other finishes it.

The same disillusioned delegate we heard from above made another ccomment on Lausanne's teaching about mutual submission in marriage: 'Ephesians 5 – where it makes clear that a wife should submit to her husband – this obvious and main message of the paragraph was not stated but was repressed. Ephesians 5.21 "submitting to one another out of reverence for Christ" was made to fight against and overcome the clear teaching of Scripture in Ephesians 5.22-24 and elsewhere. Equality was emphasized to the point that the scriptural commands were made naught, a very disturbing use of Scripture... Regarding 1Timothy 2.12a, "I do not permit a woman to teach or to exercise authority over a man", the clear teaching was repressed – not even mentioned – and suppositions were brought in to try to nullify this teaching.'[15]

The misuse of Scripture in the presentations on female leadership and mutual submission in marriage, illustrates how the leadership of Lausanne is prepared to select and twist Scripture to drive their ideological agenda. The Lausanne campaign to promote women's leadership in the Church is contrary to Scripture, which teaches an authority principle that is to be upheld in the home and the church.

The apostle Paul is clear that a woman must not have authority over a man. 'I do not permit a woman to teach or to have authority over a man' (1 Timothy 2.12). Paul appeals to the divine order of creation as support for this biblical truth—Adam was formed first and then Eve from the rib of the man, to be a suitable helper for him. He then gives a further argument, namely that it was the woman who was deceived not the man (vv13-14). The implication is that men are responsible for the teaching and preaching of sound doctrine and not women, for women are, in general, more easily deceived. Whether we like it or not Scripture teaches God's plan for male headship, just as it teaches God's plan for wives, older and younger (Titus 2.3-5). We must understand that female leadership in the Church goes hand in hand with other false doctrines. The Lausanne promotion of women's leadership is a recipe for confusion and disorder in the church and the home. The tragedy is that many churches from the Third World are being misled by Lausanne's feminist agenda.

(Endnotes)

1 The Lausanne Movement website, Document, The Manila Manifesto of 1989, affirmation 14

2 Lausanne Occasional Paper No. 30, 'Globalization and the Gospel: Rethinking Mission in the Contemporary World', produced by the Issue Group on this topic at the 2004 Forum for World Evangelization hosted by the Lausanne Committee for World Evangelization in Pattaya, Thailand, September 29 to October 5, 2004

3 The Cape Town 2010 Congress, Videos, 'Integrity - Men and Women', Author: Elke Werner, Date: 24.10.2010

4 Lausanne Global Conversation, 'The Partnership of Males and Females in the New Global Equilibrium' by Leslie Anne Neal Segraves and Chad Alan Neal Segraves, Advance paper, 09.07.2010, p2

5 Ibid.

6 Ibid.

7 The Ambiguity of 'Anthropos' by Michael D. Marlowe, 2003

8 Michael Marlowe, personal communiqué

9 The Partnership of Males and Females in the New Global Equilibrium, p5 (Ref 4 above)

10 Ibid. p5

11 Ibid. p6

12 Comment by William Lauesen, http://conversation.lausanne.org/en/conversations/detail/10557

13 Cape Town 2010 Congress, Videos, 'Men and Women: Husband and Wife Partnership', Authors, David and Robyn Claydon, http://conversation.lausanne.org/en/conversations/detail/11633

14 Ibid.

15 Comment by William Lauesen, http://conversation.lausanne.org/en/conversations/detail/10557

Chapter 11

Lausanne's environmental agenda

One of the fruits of Lausanne III was the production of The Cape Town Commitment, entitled *A Confession of Faith and a Call to Action* (2011). The Cape Town Commitment was edited by Dr Christopher Wright, chair of the Lausanne Theology Working Group. The foreword, written by Douglas Birdsall, reminds us that it 'stands in an historic line, building on both The Lausanne Covenant and The Manila Manifesto... The Cape Town Commitment will act as a roadmap for The Lausanne Movement over the next ten years. Its prophetic call to work and to pray will, we hope, draw churches, mission agencies, seminaries, Christians in the workplace, and student fellowships on campus to embrace it, and to find their part in its outworking.'[1]

The Cape Town Commitment's call to action emphasises the importance of caring for the earth. 'We care for the earth and responsibly use its abundant resources, not according to the rationale of the secular world, but for the Lord's sake. If Jesus is Lord of all the earth, we cannot separate our relationship to Christ from how we act in relation to the earth... Such love for God's creation demands that we repent of our part in the destruction, waste and pollution of the earth's resources and our collusion in the toxic idolatry of consumerism. Instead, we commit ourselves to urgent and prophetic ecological responsibility. We support Christians whose particular missional calling is to environmental advocacy and action, as well as those committed to godly fulfilment of the mandate to provide for human welfare and needs by exercising responsible dominion and stewardship.'[2]

In *Issues Facing Christians Today*, John Stott identified 'our human environment' as a key issue. He exhorted Christians 'to learn to think and act ecologically. We repent of extravagance, pollution and wanton destruction.'[3] He reminded the Cape Town Congress that the spectre of global warming was one of the big challenges facing the Church. So it was no surprise that the environment featured prominently on the Congress agenda. The emerging church movement is equally concerned—Brian McLaren identifies environmental breakdown as a global crisis 'caused by our unsustainable global economy, an economy that fails to respect environmental limits, even as it succeeds in producing great wealth for about one-third of the world's population'.[4]

The eminent British scientist, Sir John Houghton, who was the co-chair of the Nobel Peace Prize winning Intergovernmental Panel on Climate Change's (IPCC), presented what he claimed was the scientific case for global warming. He concluded with this warning: 'We're going to get more of them [floods] and they are going to be more intense. In fact, the best estimates made by scientists are that by the middle of the century the risk of floods and droughts will go up by about a factor of five—and that's very bad news indeed. The church should be seizing the opportunity because the world is desperate for leadership. We have a picture of the fragile earth, more fragile than we once thought and we have to do something about it.'[5]

An advance paper, entitled 'The Challenge of Environmental Stewardship', written by Las Newman and Ken Gnanakan provided an overview for the multiplex session devoted to the environmental crisis. Congress delegates were informed that the biblical mandate to rule and have dominion has caused the environmental disaster. Ken Gnanakan asserted that colonialism, capitalism and our Christian arrogance lay behind the ecological crisis.

The authors of the paper went on to say that 'the global environmental crisis is a stark reality that compels us to act. We are threatened with climate change, depletion of land and marine resources, dwindling fresh water reserves, an energy crunch, biodiversity extinction and devastated ecosystems... While the threat is global, sadly the impacts of the crisis are already being felt by some of the world's poorest communities. And these impacts—floods, drought, crop failure, disease and sea level rise—are escalating at an alarming rate.' The authors continue: 'We are believers in a "Creator" and a "Redeemer" God and hence have a great responsibility to act on God's behalf in our world today.'[6]

137

The authors want Christians to become environmental activists, and so they advise all Christians to commit to re-reading the Bible from an environmental perspective. In other words, we are being encouraged to reinterpret Scripture in the light of the claims of the modern-day environmental lobby. But this is the wrong way to use Scripture, for our thinking should be shaped by Scripture and not the environmental movement. Indeed, we should examine the claims of the environmental movement in the light of Scripture.

The authors advise Christians to join environmental groups and fight for change. We must make our church, Bible college, seminary, university or any other institution a vehicle for 'right teaching' about the environment. We must mobilise community awareness, education and action in our immediate communities. We must advocate alternative energy sources, encourage wise consumption patterns, ensure appropriate public transportation policies, promote a responsible tourism industry and take all other steps to make our village, town or city an ideal eco-habitation. The authors say, 'We must set up or support poverty alleviation projects of all kinds to help decrease the gap between the rich and poor', and 'in the task of world evangelization we must let the message of Jesus about how God cares for his creation speak to all about God's love for the world. Let us make Jesus to shine amidst the environmental crisis we face today.'[7]

Inconvenient truth or global warming swindle?

But the global warming issue is not as straightforward as Lausanne would have us believe, for the science behind the theory is highly controversial. Sharply different views are presented in two well publicised films. Al Gore's, *An Inconvenient Truth*, which has been shown to schoolchildren in the UK, is a passionate polemic in support of the claim that global warming, caused by an accumulation of carbon dioxide in the atmosphere, is the greatest danger facing mankind. Gore's documentary presents a computer-animated polar bear treading water, struggling to find rest on the last, thin shelf of ice which breaks apart under his weight. It is an image expressly designed to provoke emotion in the viewer. Polar bears, it would seem, are currently thriving.[8]

On the other side of the dispute is *The Great Global Warming Swindle*, a documentary shown on British television that has been viewed by millions of people on the Internet. This film claims to blow the whistle on what it says may be the biggest swindle in modern history.

An Inconvenient Truth is advertised as 'a passionate and inspirational look at former Vice-President Al Gore's fervent crusade to halt global warming's deadly progress by exposing the myths and misconceptions that surround it... With an emphasis on hope, *An Inconvenient Truth* ultimately shows us that global warming is no longer a political issue but rather, the biggest moral challenge facing our civilization today.'[9] While the film won plaudits from the environmental lobby and an Oscar from the film industry, it was found wanting when a father challenged the biased presentation of scientific facts presented to school children. In a judicial review in the High Court in London, Judge Michael Burton identified nine significant errors within the documentary film. He said some of the claims made by the film were wrong and had arisen in the context of alarmism and exaggeration.[10] He pointed out that the apocalyptic vision presented in the film was politically partisan and not an impartial analysis of the science of climate change.

Here are three of the nine errors mentioned by the judge. First, Al Gore's assertion that a sea level rise of up to 20 feet would be caused by melting of ice in either West Antarctica or Greenland 'in the near future' was 'distinctly alarmist'. Second, the assertion that the disappearance of snow on Mount Kilimanjaro in East Africa was expressly attributable to global warming was not supported by scientific consensus. Third, reference to a new scientific study showing that, for the first time, polar bears had actually drowned 'swimming long distances – up to 60 miles – to find the ice' was not supported by evidence. The judge said: 'The only scientific study that either side before me can find is one which indicates that four polar bears have recently been found drowned because of a storm.'[11]

The Great Global Warming Swindle, which claims to be the definitive rebuttal to Al Gore's film, 'examines the mass of observational data (from temperature balloons, weather satellites, ocean temperature data, ice core records and much else besides) which directly contradict the popular theory of man-made global warming. It features testimony from many senior scientists, describing both the fatal weaknesses in the theory of man-made global warming, and their failed attempts to bring these to public attention.' While humans have an effect on climate, it is but 'an infinitesimally small pin-prick, compared with the vast natural forces which have always, and are still constantly pushing global temperatures this way and that'.[12] The film 'describes how a fashionable prejudice was elevated to the status of unquestionable scientific fact. It shows how, in an age we consider rational, reason can descend into dogma. Global warming is indeed the biggest threat facing the world today, but not in the way you think.'[13]

Cornwall Alliance for the stewardship of creation

The Cornwall Alliance is a coalition of clergy, theologians, religious leaders, scientists, academics, and policy experts committed to bringing a balanced biblical view of stewardship to the critical issues of environment and development. In 2009, the Alliance issued 'An Evangelical Declaration on Global Warming' to challenge the propaganda of the global warning lobby: 'As governments consider policies to fight alleged man-made global warming, evangelical leaders have a responsibility to be well informed, and then to speak out.' The declaration refers to its detailed paper on global warming, entitled 'A Renewed Call to Truth, Prudence, and Protection of the Poor: An Evangelical Examination of the Theology, Science, and Economics of Global Warming', which 'demonstrates that many of these proposed policies would destroy jobs and impose trillions of dollars in costs to achieve no net benefits. They could be implemented only by enormous and dangerous expansion of government control over private life. Worst of all, by raising energy prices and hindering economic development, they would slow or stop the rise of the world's poor out of poverty and so condemn millions to premature death.'[14]

The Alliance denies 'that Earth and its ecosystems are the fragile and unstable products of chance, and particularly that Earth's climate system is vulnerable to dangerous alteration because of minuscule changes in atmospheric chemistry. Recent warming was neither abnormally large nor abnormally rapid. There is no convincing scientific evidence that human contribution to greenhouse gases is causing dangerous global warming.'[15]

The Alliance also denies 'that carbon dioxide—essential to all plant growth—is a pollutant. Reducing greenhouse gases cannot achieve significant reductions in future global temperatures, and the costs of the policies would far exceed the benefits.'[16]

Dr E. Calvin Beisner, a spokesman for the Cornwall Alliance and a former Associate Professor of Historical Theology and Social Ethics at Knox Theological Seminary in Fort Lauderdale, Florida, having examined the economic side-effects of anti-CO_2 policies, reaches the following conclusion: 'The policies that are being promoted to fight global warming not only will not make a difference... but also will have a great harmful impact on the world's poor.'[17] According to Beisner, even the vast changes proposed by global warming activists would have only a negligible effect on CO_2 levels in the atmosphere, with little possibility of reversing or even slowing global warming. But if the proposed changes become reality, the potential costs in lives and freedoms would be incalculable.[18]

Environmentalism and the humanist agenda

So where does the truth lie? Lausanne has come down firmly on the side of Al Gore, but fails to acknowledge that environmentalism is a central tenet of secular humanism. Moreover, Lausanne's position on climate change is entirely consistent with that of the United Nations, which has taken the lead in the fight against global warming. In 2007, the Nobel Peace Prize was awarded jointly to former US Vice-President, Al Gore, and the UN Intergovernmental Panel on Climate Change (IPCC), 'for their efforts to build up and disseminate greater knowledge about man-made climate change, and to lay the foundations for the measures that are needed to counteract such change'.[19]

The International and Humanist Ethical Union, like Lausanne, 'believes that action to halt environmental destruction must include education at all levels about the problems of pollution and waste of resources, so that this knowledge becomes common property'.[20] Humanists see themselves as being in control of 'our planet' and campaign vigorously for humankind to join together to save the planet from untimely destruction caused by climate change. Behind such thinking is an idolatrous attitude and pantheistic vision that worships the creation and ignores the Creator (Romans 1). This idolatry, which is manifest in the idea that mankind has the power to 'save our planet', ignores the biblical truth that 'the earth is the LORD's, and all its fullness, the world and those who dwell therein' (Psalm 24.1).

God controls the climate

Scripture tells us that God has created the world to be populated and used by mankind. Men and women, created in the image of God, are commanded to have dominion over God's creation. The earth and its rich resources have been created by God for man (the only creature created in the image of God) to develop and use. And the resources of God's world are sufficient to supply the needs of mankind.

The people of God, who read and study Scripture, understand their God-given responsibility to be good stewards of the earth. They know that mankind was given dominion over all creation, and is responsible for taking care of it (Genesis 1.26; 2.15; Psalm 8.6-8). They also know that Scripture teaches that God is in control of the climate. The Lord Jesus said, 'Your Father in heaven… makes His sun rise on the evil and on the good, and sends rain on the just and on the unjust' (Matthew 5.45). The book of Job declares that God controls the weather. 'God thunders marvellously with His voice; He does great things which we cannot comprehend. For He says to the snow, "Fall on the earth"; likewise to the gentle rain and the heavy rain of His strength"' (Job 37.5-6). Job continues: 'From the chamber of the south comes the whirlwind and cold from the scattering winds of the north. By the breath of God ice is given and the broad waters are frozen. Also with moisture He saturates the thick clouds; He scatters His bright clouds. And they swirl about, being turned by His guidance, that they may do whatever He commands them on the face of the whole earth' (Job 37.9-12). God not only controls the weather and the climate, but man cannot even pretend to understand how and why he does so. 'Do you know how the clouds are balanced, those wondrous works of Him who is perfect in knowledge?' (Job 37.16).

God has promised that, 'While the earth remains, seedtime and harvest, cold and heat, winter and summer, and day and night shall not cease' (Genesis 8.22). It follows that man does not have the power to appreciably alter the climate. Scripture is clear that the heavens and earth are now preserved by the Word of God (2 Peter 3.7)—reserved for fire when 'the elements will melt with fervent heat; both the earth and the works that are in it will be burned up' (v10) at the Lord's return. This earth, which is passing away to be replaced by a new heaven and earth (Revelation 21.1-2), is governed by God, who alone controls the climate and who alone knows when the end of time will come.

'An Evangelical Declaration on Global Warming', mentioned above declares: 'We believe Earth and its ecosystems – created by God's intelligent design and infinite power and sustained by His faithful providence – are robust, resilient, self-regulating, and self-correcting, admirably suited for human flourishing, and displaying His glory. Earth's climate system is no exception. Recent global warming is one of many natural cycles of warming and cooling in geologic history.'

While Christians are to be good stewards of God's creation, we should not allow politically-driven hysteria to dominate our view of the environment. Lausanne's vehement support for the global warming lobby, placing itself alongside Al Gore and the UN Intergovernmental Panel on Climate Change (IPCC), is further evidence of how far the Lausanne Movement has strayed from biblical truth.

(Endnotes)

1 The Cape Town Commitment: A Confession of Faith and a Call to Action (2011), Foreword

2 Ibid. paragraph 7, 'We love God's world'

3 John Stott, *Issues Facing Christians Today*, Marshall Pickering, 1990, p126

4 Brian McLaren, *Everything must change*, Thomas Nelson, 2007, p5

5 Cape Town 2010 Congress video, 'The Environmental Crisis' - Presentation 1, Author: Dr John Houghton, Date: 23.10.2010

6 The Lausanne Global Conversation, Cape Town 2010 advance paper, 'The Challenge Of Environmental Stewardship', Authors: Las Newman and Ken Gnanakan, Date: 29.07.2010, p1

7 Ibid. p2

8 Answers in Genesis magazine, article 'Global warming in perspective' part 4, by Melinda Christian, Oct–Dec. 2008, p87, http://www.answersingenesis.org/contents/379/am/v3/n4/global-warming.pdf

9 Climate Crisis website, The Film, http://www.climatecrisis.net/an_inconvenient_truth/about_the_film.php

10 The Times October 11, 2007, 'Al Gore's inconvenient judgment', Lewis Smith, Environment Reporter

11 Gore climate film's nine 'errors', BBC News channel, Thursday, 11 October 2007

12 The Great Global Warming Swindle website,, http://www.wagtv.com/programme/The-Great-Global-Warming-Swindle-316.html

13 Ibid.

14 Cornwall Alliance website, An Evangelical Declaration on Global Warming, http://www.cornwallalliance.org/articles/read/an-evangelical-declaration-on-global-warming/

15 Ibid.

16 Ibid.

17 D. James Kennedy and E. Calvin Beisner, Overheated: A Reasoned Look at the Global Warming Debate (Ft. Lauderdale, Florida: Coral Ridge Ministries, 2007), p23.

18 Answers in Genesis magazine, article 'Global warming in perspective', p88 (Ref 8 above)

19 Nobel Prize website, The Nobel Peace Prize 2007, Intergovernmental Panel on Climate Change , Al Gore

20 International and Humanist Ethical Union website, UN conference on the human environment, Submitted by admin on 9 August, 1970, Environment United Nations news, Resolutions & statements, http://www.iheu.org/node/2026

Chapter 12

Lausanne's socio-political agenda

Bishop Frank Retief, Presiding Bishop of the Church of England in South Africa, was fulsome in his praise of the third Lausanne Congress. In an article in *Evangelicals Now*, he wrote that the final service dispelled any doubts that may have lingered about where Lausanne has gone theologically. The closing message by Lindsay Brown, the International Director for the Lausanne Movement, 'was magnificent and gave a clarion call to the historical Reformed evangelical faith – the uniqueness of Christ, the importance of the cross, the lostness of people, the preaching of the gospel, the need for conversion. I am aware that there is always a push for the "main thing" to be sidelined. But thank God the main thing remained the main thing at Lausanne'.[1]

So the Bishop endorsed the Congress as faithfully proclaiming the Reformed faith and the uniqueness of the Cross. Having observed the Congress described in these pages, the Bishop declared to the evangelical world that all is well with Lausanne. But the Bishop, although clearly sincere, has been deceived and is misleading the evangelical world, for Lausanne has not proclaimed the Reformed faith, but seems intent on destroying it. In chapter four we saw Douglas Birdsall's memo published in *Lausanne World Pulse* (December 2010): 'It is my hope in 2020 that the evangelical Church will make progress in its relationships with the historic churches of the Christian faith. It is in this same spirit of humility and integrity that we must extend the hand of fellowship to the Catholic, Orthodox, and Ecumenical Church.'[2]

False ecumenism

The Fundamental Evangelistic Association, unlike the Presiding Bishop of the Church of England in South Africa, has not been taken in by Lausanne. Two decades ago, having observed the second Lausanne

Congress in Manila and using spiritual discernment, the Association warned that 'the ecumenical, unbiblical concept of the "wholeness of the gospel" makes the Lausanne Covenant a springboard for all sorts of strange things – social action, feminist theology, ecumenism, charismatic confusion, compromised fellowships, unbalanced missions programs. All can find their supposed justification by quoting some portion of the Covenant.'[3]

Before Cape Town 2010, the covert aim of Lausanne's ecumenical agenda was to slowly move evangelical Christians to the doors of Rome. The co-founders, Billy Graham and John Stott, were working over the years to remove the barriers to this reunion. The Lausanne cry for 'unity in love' is, in reality, a cry for the 'separated evangelical brothers and sisters' identified by Vatican II to rejoin the Mother Church in Rome. While this aim was not openly stated prior to Cape Town, for not all in the Lausanne Movement were ready to submit to papal authority, this was the direction of travel. Those who continue to go along with Lausanne's ecumenical agenda ultimately place themselves under the spiritual authority of the Bishop of Rome.

Cape Town 2010 provided a vivid picture of ecumenical confusion. It showed that the ever closer unity of evangelicals with every other brand of 'Christianity', no matter how unbiblical, no matter how compromised, is gathering momentum. We saw how the Alpha Course, which openly works with the Roman Catholic Church, was given a platform to promote its ecumenical agenda. Nicky Gumbel made an impassioned plea for Protestants and Catholics to stop fighting each other, for 'what unites us is infinitely greater than what divides us'.[4]

There is no doubt that the Lausanne leadership is comfortable with the liberal ideology of the World Council of Churches, the excesses of the charismatic movement, the ecumenical and deficient 'gospel' of the Alpha Course, the false teachings of Roman Catholicism, and the new ideas and methods of the emerging church. The evidence in this book demonstrates that Lausanne has turned its back on the doctrines of the Reformation.

But the ecumenical passion that drives Lausanne does nothing to protect God's people from false teaching that seeks to pervert the Gospel of truth, and robs the lost of the opportunity of hearing the authentic soul-saving Gospel of the Lord Jesus Christ.

Low view of Scripture

At the heart of the Lausanne Movement is the downgrade of Scripture. While the Lausanne Covenant affirms that Scripture is 'the only written Word of God, without error in all that it affirms, and the only infallible rule of faith and practice', we should note that this affirmation, which is virtually the same as that of Fuller Theological Seminary, allows for error in the arenas of science and history. In other words, it is a view of Scripture that opens the door to errors like theistic evolution, as we saw with John Stott. Lausanne is so careless in its use of Scripture that it eagerly promotes the concept of an 'oral story Bible' made up of stories crafted to be culturally relevant and worldview sensitive.

The Lausanne Movement is skilled at using Scripture to support its socio-political agenda. We have seen how Scripture is twisted to support a feminist agenda. In the session on marriage at the Cape Town 2010 Congress, verses from Ephesians 5 that referred to headship of the husband and submission of the wife were simply ignored, creating the false impression that Scripture teaches that marriage is an equal-regard relationship based on mutual submission. Taken in the round, the socio-political agenda of the Lausanne Movement pays little more than lip-service to Scripture.

High view of the arts

While Lausanne has a low view of Scripture, like the emerging church, it has a high view of the arts. The opening and closing ceremonies at Cape Town were musical extravaganzas that sought to integrate worship with the arts. The visual arts and drama dominated the Congress. The idea that the message of Ephesians 2 can be illuminated by four people prancing around the Congress stage to the 'dark and dangerous' sounds of 'Dirty Pool' is surely indicative of the spirit of Lausanne. The sight of four thousand Christians enjoying trivial dramatic presentations says much about how very far Lausanne has moved from the Reformed faith based on the sufficiency of Scripture.

The orality movement

The ultimate compromise of Lausanne is its promotion of the orality movement and the so-called oral Bible. Consistent with its low view

147

of Scripture and high view of the Roman Catholic Church, Lausanne has eagerly embraced the thinking of Walter Ong, a Jesuit priest who asserts that the spoken word is a medium superior to the written word. The premise that the truth of God is contained and best conveyed in crafted Bible stories is ridiculous. The assertion that so-called 'oral preferenced learners' (those who prefer not to read) need to hear stories rather than the written Word of God comes from the wisdom of man that is foolishness in the sight of God.

Distorted view of Christ's Great Commission

The socialist ideology of John Stott and Ronald Sider has, to a large extent, shaped the ministry of the Lausanne Movement. Stott believed that proclamation of the Gospel and social action goes together like 'two wings of a bird.'[5] So Lausanne is promoting the idea that the Church's Great Commission has two wings—faith in Christ and socio-political action. But this is a distorted view of the Great Commission, based on the 'wisdom' of John Stott, not on Scripture. In Matthew's Gospel, the risen Lord Jesus instructs his disciples to baptize all nations in the name of the Father, Son, and Holy Spirit (Matthew 28.19-20). In Luke's Gospel, Christ tells his disciples to preach repentance and remission of sins in his name among all nations (Luke 24.47).

But Lausanne downplays the idea that the real problem of mankind is sin in the human heart, while focussing on the problems of political oppression, poverty and social injustice. It follows that salvation is freedom from oppression, liberation from social injustice and the alleviation of poverty by the redistribution of wealth. The ambition of World Vision to redistribute wealth from the rich Global North to the poor Global South is an important dimension of Lausanne's socio-political agenda.

Lausanne's two winged version of the Great Commission (evangelism and socio-political action) is contrary to Scripture, for Christ is not a socio-political revolutionary, but the Lamb of God who takes away the sin of the world. He came to call sinners to repentance, not to call for the redistribution of the world's resources. 'This is a faithful saying and worthy of all acceptance: Christ Jesus came into the world to save sinners' (1 Timothy 1.15). The fault line in Lausanne's approach is that it has turned the Church aside to socio-political endeavours; this means that the crucial work of the Great Commission to go into all the world and preach the gospel of Christ is being undermined (Mark 16.15).

Feminist agenda

One of the central aims of Lausanne is the feminisation of the Church. The cardinal idea of feminism within the Church, that women must have equal authority with men in church leadership, was eagerly promoted by the Cape Town Congress. It follows that Lausanne wants women to be pastors, preachers and church leaders. Another aspect of the feminist agenda is equal-regard marriage (mutual submission), and the consequent denial of the headship role of the husband in marriage and the family. The contrast between God's prescription of headship in his Word and the feminist agenda at Lausanne could not be more stark.

Environmental agenda

According to Lausanne the so-called ecological crisis has been caused by capitalism, colonialism and the arrogance of Western Christians. Lausanne's deep commitment to the concept of climate change is simply an aspect of its socialist agenda. This approach is consistent with the ideology of secular humanism and the ecological agenda of the United Nations. It must surely be of great concern that Lausanne's position on global warming is similar to that of Al Gore, and in direct opposition to 'An Evangelical Declaration on Global Warming', discussed in chapter 11. If Lausanne were truly a Christian organisation then it would diligently seek to understand the truth about the claims being made by the global warming lobby. Rather than blindly following the propaganda promoted by Al Gore and his friends in the global warming industry, Christians need to exercise spiritual discernment and test the spirits to see whether they are of God. Lausanne's passionate promotion of climate change propaganda is misleading the Church.

Tragedy of the Lausanne compromise

The corrupt fruit of the Lausanne Movement has been produced by the coming together of the ecumenical movement, the compromise of the new evangelicals (led by Billy Graham and John Stott) and the false teaching of the emerging church. Lausanne's compromise, so vividly illustrated at Cape Town 2010, is the true legacy of the worldwide ministries of Billy Graham and John Stott.

When Billy Graham, as a world famous evangelist, embraced the compromise of new evangelicalism in the 1950s and 60s, he opened the door to a liberal theological agenda. He used his very considerable reputation and influence to enable Fuller Theological Seminary, a deeply compromised institution, to act as a driving force behind the Lausanne agenda. Over the decades, Fuller Seminary has eagerly grasped the opportunity offered by Lausanne to promote its compromised theological ideas to the world. Fuller's church growth strategy has succeeded in changing the focus of the Great Commission of Matthew 28 from preaching the Gospel of salvation, to a people's movement that aims primarily to redeem cultures, not to save individual souls.

John Stott, as a world famous theologian, must have been well aware of the theological corruption within Fuller Seminary, yet he chose to walk the same road. He undoubtedly understood the significance of the orality movement in downgrading Scripture, yet he endorsed the Cape Town Congress, knowing full well that the promotion of the orality movement was presented as a strategic priority. Stott never opposed Lausanne's commitment to an oral story Bible. Over the years he used the Lausanne Movement as a vehicle for promoting his socio-political ideology to the Third World.

Lausanne III stands as a theological disaster perpetrated in the name of new evangelicalism, and driven by the deeply flawed ministries of John Stott and Billy Graham. The tragedy of Lausanne is that it brings together true believers, mainly from developing African and Asian countries, with false teachers, mainly from the West. It is deeply disturbing that genuine believers from growing churches in the Third World are being profoundly influenced by the false teachings of the Lausanne Movement.

In the light of the evidence presented in this study, we must conclude that Lausanne is a heretical movement that is perverting the Gospel of truth. Its oral Bible cannot remotely measure up to God's written Word revealed in Scripture—rather, it perverts the Word of Truth. Its socio-political message is a false utopian gospel based on the ideology of socialism. The Lausanne Movement simply does not contend for the Gospel of truth once for all delivered to the saints.

The true Gospel is the power of God unto salvation to everyone who believes in Christ and repents of sin. True believers are born from above by the work of the Holy Spirit. We are adopted into God's family and become God's children. We receive the righteousness of Christ and have peace with God. We are justified (made right with God) by faith in Christ alone. It is God's will that believers, with the help of the Holy Spirit, should strive for holiness, and through obedience to God's Word, be sanctified and increasingly transformed into the image of Christ. As Christ's disciples true believers are to seek to obey his commands, to deny themselves and take up their cross daily. Sincere believers, those who would be true to the Gospel of Christ, need to separate themselves from the deception of the Lausanne Movement, for what fellowship has righteousness with unrighteousness? (2 Corinthians 6.14-15).

Moreover, true believers should not only separate from Lausanne, they should be prepared to give the reasons for doing so in order to warn others who are being deceived. It is especially important that Christian believers in the Third World are protected from the savage wolves that lie behind the Lausanne Movement.

Our Lord said that his sheep follow him, for they know his voice. The stranger they will not follow, but will flee from him (John 10.4-5). So, true believer, flee the Lausanne compromise.

(Endnotes)

1 *Evangelicals Now*, December 2010, article by Bishop Frank Retief, 'Lausanne: the main thing'

2 *Lausanne World Pulse*, December 2010, 'Pressing on towards 2020 in Humility, Reflection, and Hope' by Douglas Birdsall, http://www.lausanneworldpulse.com/pdf/issues/December2010PDF2.pdf

3 Source: Fundamental Evangelistic Association, Lausanne II in Manila, cited from the website of 'The Global Prayer & Missions Movement Database, Strategic Partnerships for the Propagation of Another Gospel', http://watch.pair.com/gpm-missions.html#lausanne

4 *Alpha News*, March-June 2004, p7

5 John Stott, *The Contemporary Christian*, Intervarsity Press, 1992, pp339-40

47949883R00088

Made in the USA
Middletown, DE
11 June 2019